~~~~~~~~~

TECHNIQUES
OF
TROUT FISHING
AND
FLY TYING

~~~~~~~~~

Techniques
of
TROUT FISHING
and
FLY TYING

GEORGE W. HARVEY

Lyons & Burford, Publishers

To my wife, Helen,
for her constant and unwavering support

The Publishers warmly thank Buck Metz and the Metz Hatchery for kind permission to reprint material from their edition of *Techniques of Trout Fishing and Fly Tying*. Metz Hatchery (P.O. Box 5666, Belleville, PA 17004) produces premium necks for fly tying.

Printed in the United States of America
10 9 8 7 6 5 4 3

Library of Congress Cataloging-in-Publication Data

Harvey, George W.
    Techniques of trout fishing and fly tying / George W. Harvey.
        p.   cm.
    "Nick Lyons books."
    Originally published: Belleville, PA. : Metz Hatchery, 1985.
    ISBN 1-55821-068-7 —ISBN 1-55821-074-1 (pbk.)
    1. Fly fishing. 2. Fly tying. 3. Trout fishing. I. Title.
SH456.H33   1990
799.1'755—dc20   89-77187
                                                       CIP

Contents

INTRODUCTION
To The First Edition

~~~~~~~~~

EVER since that venerable English prioress of the fifteenth century, Dame Juliana Berners, popularized fly tying as an art form, there have been many master fly tyers. Whether men or women (and a lot were women) they have always been adjudged such by three criteria: the effectiveness, the originality, or the inherent beauty of their flies.

George Harvey qualifies as a master fly tyer in all three categories and a fourth as well, one in which he is without peer, that of fly-tying instructor. There is no question but that George has taught more people to tie trout flies than anyone on record.

In 1973 George retired after thirty-eight years as associate professor and head of required physical education for men at Pennsylvania State University, where he instructed over 35,000 youngsters and adults in angling, casting, and fly tying. In 1934 he organized and taught the first angling and fly-tying classes (non credit) in the United States (at Penn State). The first accredited university-level angling course in the country was given there by George in 1947.

A longtime contributor to fishing publications, George has advised various tackle companies, continuously instructed in Pennsylvania's leading fly-fishing schools, conducted forty-two angling clinics, and taught seventy-two extension classes. He received the coveted Order of the Hat from the Harrisburg Fly Fishers Club, the Buz Buszek award from the Federation of Fly Fishers, and the Award of Merit from the American

Association of Conservation Information for his outstanding career in teaching anglers and conservation. He fished with and tied flies for both President Eisenhower and President Carter.

George's career as a fly-tying instructor is significant for a reason more important than qualifying for the Guinness Book of Records. If trout and pure water are to survive the encroachments of expanding human populations, we must have more fly anglers to promote the cause, for fly anglers are able to conserve fish and they require top-quality water to permit use of their fur and feathered imitations. By creating a literal army of fly-angler lobbyists, George has contributed monumentally to the cause of trout and water conservation.

Perhaps George Harvey's first instructional booklet was responsible for teaching as many fly tyers as were his classes. Certainly his "easy as falling off a log" graphic course (done for the Pennsylvania Fish Commission) was widely disseminated far beyond the borders of the Keystone State. This new, updated, and improved edition will surely be responsible for introducing many more anglers and potential anglers to the most satisfying and rewarding of pastimes, the art of fly tying and fly fishing.

If you are about to approach a vise and bobbin for the first time, you can have no more effective teacher by your side than this book. It is my pleasure to recommend it highly, without qualification.

—S.R. SLAYMAKER II
1985

One

Techniques
of
Fly Fishing

1

Fly Fishing

~~~~~~~~~~

FLY fishing, for any species that will take an artificial fly, is the most challenging, enjoyable, exciting yet exasperating individual sport in the world today. There are so many techniques to master that one who spends a lifetime with the sport can always learn something new.

When I first started fly fishing in 1917, fly fishermen, in fact fishermen of any kind, were few and far between. You could fish day after day and never have any competition. In those days anyone who approached a pool carefully and cast or dapped a fly on the surface could take trout. It was much easier then to take a day's limit (twenty-five) than it is today. Practically all of the trout were brookies and quite easy to catch. It was an occasion to catch a brown trout, in fact I was twelve years old before I caught my first!

With the ever-increasing number of fishermen and the stocking of legal-sized trout, many techniques that used to take trout are worthless. In our heavily fished waters, the stream-bred fish become extremely shy and cautious. Even the hatchery trout that are not caught within the first few days after planting become pretty cagey and are more difficult to take than the native brookies I fished for as a youngster. If today one used the equipment I started with, he would be lucky to catch a single trout. We have advanced so much in knowledge and equipment that today's anglers really have it made. The tackle manufacturers are continually striving through research to improve their products; as a result today's fishermen have the finest equipment that can possibly be manufactured. Fine fishing tackle in itself cannot make a fly fisherman, but it can surely speed up the process. It should be recognized that skilled craftsmen usually have the finest tools they can afford, and the tool of the angler is his tackle.

I want everyone who reads what follows to know I am still experimenting and always learning something new. What I have learned and know about fly fishing for trout is a result of having probably spent more hours astream than anyone else my age, being involved in trout research, observing fish behavior, and being taught by the best teacher, the trout.

Many fly anglers, once they learn to cast and tie on a fly, progress very little beyond this point. Sure, they catch a few trout and are probably satisfied, but instead of learning something new every day astream, their observations are static.

I know of many such anglers who have fished for years and believe they have had years of experience, when all they really have is the first year's experience repeated over and over.

If one is to derive the fullest enjoyment from the sport, in order to be able to fish throughout the season, under all water conditions, he must be a complete angler. He must assimilate as much knowledge as possible in the techniques of fishing dry, wet, nymph, bucktail, and streamer flies. Millions of words have been written about this fascinating sport. Sadly, much that has been written has discouraged many budding anglers from attempting to take fish on artificial flies.

For some unknown reason many writers greatly exaggerate the skills involved in various techniques and actually give the reader the impression fly fishing is difficult to master and that he must possess supernatural intelligence and skill to catch fish by this method. This is a fallacy! I have taught more people to tie flies, cast, and fly fish for trout than anyone else in the United States. At this writing, the number is approximately 35,000. I have had hundreds of students who, in as few as ten class periods, have learned to cast, tie their own flies, and catch trout on their own creations the first time they were on the stream.

Anyone can learn to catch trout if he or she will take time to learn to cast well enough to present a fly in the proper manner. The quickest way to become a proficient caster is to acquire the services of a competent instructor. As soon as one learns to cast, he should be able to catch trout consistently if he just uses good common sense, has proper equipment, and spends enough time on a stream to learn the simple fundamentals and techniques that will be described in the following pages.

It stands to reason one must have a basic knowledge of the habits, peculiarities, and survival instincts of the species he pursues. This is most important yet is disregarded by many anglers. Stream-bred and even hatchery trout that are fished over constantly become very shy creatures and are increasingly more difficult to take as the season advances. This is especially true on streams that become low and clear. The majority of the early season trouters give up at this time of the year because they cannot catch trout, but the devoted angler waits for this period because the streams are practically free from competition. The successful anglers who are fishing then are the ones who have learned by experience how to approach and present a fly correctly to a feeding trout. I feel it is the most enjoyable part of the whole season and anyone who is a keen observer and really wants to improve his chance of success should spend as much time as possible on a stream at this time of the year.

Water Temperature

It is surprising how many trout fishermen do not have the slightest knowledge of the importance water temperature has on the sport of trout fishing. A stream or river that will support trout throughout its length early in the season may change drastically as the season advances. This change occurs because of low water and high air temperature. This condition warms up the water to such a high degree that trout must migrate to survive.

There is no set time for this to occur because it varies in different watersheds and locations, but usually occurs by early or midsummer. A lack of such knowledge may mean many wasted hours and even days of valuable fishing time.

Back in the mid-nineteen-thirties I worked three summers from May to September on a research project studying the effect of water temperature on the migration and feeding of trout. What I write will hold true for trout wherever they are found. In the next few paragraphs I will try to give you enough general information to help prevent you from making the more common mistakes concerning trout and water temperature.

We will discuss only the three most common species: brook (char), brown, and rainbow trout. Generally speaking, the ideal temperature for brook trout is close to 58°F. and for brown and rainbow trout a few degrees higher. The optimum temperature range for the three species is about ten degrees above and below the ideal temperature. Thus, when water temperatures drop below 48° or reach above 70°F., fishing for brook trout is generally poor. In some streams in the heavily oxygenated areas it may be possible to catch brook trout in water slightly higher than 70°, but from experience I would never choose to fish in water this warm because I know my chances of taking brook trout would be reduced.

With brown and rainbow trout the situation is the same, with the optimum temperature range from about 50° to 73°. I have caught brown and rainbow trout in water as high as 75°, but I would never fish by choice in water over 70° or below 45° for any of the three species. After making thousands of temperature checks over a period of forty-eight years I am thoroughly convinced the best temperature range for all fly fishing is from 55° to 68°F.

I will admit there are exceptions. In heavily oxygenated water, the trout may live and feed in temperatures four or five degrees higher; the same is true when the water is much colder. On a few occasions I have had excellent fishing when the water temperature was in the thirties, but as a general rule this is rare.

The observant angler who repeatedly fishes the streams in his area learns by experience the effect water temperature has on the feeding and migration of the trout. If you like to explore new water, a thermometer is a must. During a normal year on all marginal streams I have fished in Pennsylvania, the first two weeks of June is the critical period when trout are forced to migrate. The time may vary as much as a month or more because of elevation or location. It is during this period that I have seen hundreds of anglers fishing in water that could not possibly support trout. The brook-trout migration usually takes place when the temperature rises above 70° and holds for a period of four or five hours a day. The same is true of browns and rainbows when the temperature gets above 75°, but when the brooks start to migrate, a good proportion of the browns and rainbows in the same stream follow. When the mass migration occurs, sections of a stream that held a good population of trout may in just a few days be completely barren except at the mouth of small cold-water tributaries, spring holes, and heavily oxygenated areas. Some of the most exciting fishing of the year may be experienced just prior to the mass migration. When the water temperatures first start reaching the 70-degree mark and hold for only a few hours a day, trout start to bunch up in the riffly or heavily oxygenated water at the heads of long flat stretches. When this happens, trout that were more or less evenly distributed over many surface acres of water are now confined to a very small area. I have on many occasions been able to cast over hundreds of trout without changing my position. Usually, the best fishing will occur late in the day when the temperature starts to drop. You will find this happening on all marginal water every year. It should be noted that on many of our streams, trout cannot migrate to ideal water because of low water, beaver dams, man-made dams, and other obstructions. In these situations the trout are forced to stay in water warmer than they prefer.

The following is a vivid example of how knowledge or lack of it can affect your fishing.

I had two stations on Kettle Creek in north-central Pennsylvania where I had placed high-low thermometers permanently in the stream from early May to September. These thermometers allowed me to check the daily, weekly, and seasonal fluctuations in water temperature. One was in the riffly area in front of the headquarters cabin, the other above the junction of Hammersley Fork and Kettle Creek.

One Friday evening the last week in May I stood in one place in front of the cabin and caught a limit of trout to take home to my family. At this time the trout were concentrated in the riffly or heavily oxygenated water prior to mass migration. When I returned early the following Monday I immediately checked the thermometer at the headquarters cabin station, because Sunday had been very hot, and found the temperature had been up to 85° during my absence.

I went to the cabin and returned with my fly rod. I made fifteen or twenty casts with no results except one or two small bass. I then headed for the Hammersley Fork station, approximately three and a half or four miles upstream. I should add that this was the first sizable tributary that entered the main stream. There were two other small wet-weather trickles between the two stations but they were dry. I parked the car and walked down to the confluence of the two streams and could hardly believe my eyes. Below, in the first fifty feet of cool water there were at least fifteen hundred trout. They were the trout that had migrated up from above Trout Run, a distance of about five miles.

On the following Saturday evening I was again checking the thermometer at the Hammersley Fork station and glanced downstream and saw two fishermen working toward me. I sat down on a log and waited for them to come up. We greeted one another and then I asked the question "How did you do?" The answer I knew but I wanted to hear it from them. They had not caught a single trout. They could not believe it because they had fished the same stretch of water two weeks before and had excellent results.

Both fishermen were from the Pittsburgh area, had the finest equipment money could buy, and were excellent casters. They were two tired and disappointed anglers!

I invited them to sit down, introduced myself, and told them about the research project I was working on.

They had never noticed the trout congregated at the mouth of Hammersley Fork and when I told them migration had occurred the previous weekend and that there were no trout in the area they had fished they could hardly believe this was true.

I then said, "If you would like to see some of the trout that you didn't catch on your last excursion, walk over and look below Hammersley Fork in Kettle Creek." They did, and I can't write the words that came from their mouths! I then explained what had taken place and how important a thermometer is at this time of the season. If they had known, they could have checked the water temperature after ten o'clock in the morning and moved upstream until they found water with a temperature of 70° or below, or fished one of the tributaries and had good fishing the rest of that day.

In the freestone streams among the mountains of north-central Pennsylvania it frequently will get quite cool during the night even during the warm summer months and the water temperature in the morning may be in the sixties. On a normal summer day when the sun gets up over the mountains it is usually about ten o'clock before the stream temperature gets above 70°. If one were fishing a stream for the first time and took the temperature in the early morning, it would be easy to be misled. This is why you must check after ten o'clock. This will hold true on any marginal stream regardless of geographical location if the nights get cool.

There is another situation one must be aware of when fishing new waters. A typical example was Hammersley Fork. There was a mile stretch of the most beautiful water one could ever wish to fish in the center section of the stream, but late in June during low water was barren of trout because the temperature would get up into the high seventies and low eighties. Above and below this stretch the water rarely got above 72°. When it did, it only held over for an hour or two a day, not long enough to cause mass migration. At the lower end of this stretch a cold tributary flowed into the center of a beautiful pool. The water in this pool all looked the same but above the junction the temperature got up to the high seventies and low eighties. One could catch brook trout up to where the tributary entered, but above that point never catch a trout.

It is important how and where you take your temperature readings. The thermometer should be held close to the bottom in a riffly or fast-moving section of the stream for at least three minutes. You must have an accurate thermometer or your readings may be worthless. I have seen some that were off by as much as three degrees, and this could make a tremendous difference in your fishing plan.

Spring Holes

In all marginal water one can usually find spring holes where trout will congregate when water temperatures get high enough to cause migration. Of course, trout will congregate at the mouths of cold-water tributaries and visible springs that flow into the main stream. If the water is clear one can easily see the trout. Springs may flow out from the bottom of the stream and if they are in deep pools where one cannot see the bottom they can be difficult to find.

One can be suspicious if the stream runs in against a moist rock ledge and gouges out a deep pool. If you check the water temperature above the pool, then check it as it leaves the pool on the side of the ledge and find the temperature cooler (one degree or more), you can be sure you have located a spring hole.

On several occasions I have found spring holes where small wet-weather tributaries entered the main stream, and at times below a dry hollow. Whenever you have ledges running across the stream with a pool below, you may find a spring.

I have taken many large trout from the previously mentioned situations and when I find one, I selfishly keep it to myself. You will have a "honey hole" only as long as the water runs pure and some angler who kills doesn't find it.

Many of our once-prime trout streams and lakes have suffered from acid rain and can no longer support trout. If you are a roving angler it would be on the side of wisdom to know if acid rain has affected the stream you wish to fish. Water temperature can be perfect but when the pH is below five, the stream has a severe problem. There are quite a few small brook-trout streams I once fished that no longer support trout and there are streams that once were excellent trout producers that the Pennsylvania Fish Commission no longer stocks. A kit to determine the pH of the water you intend to fish may be even more important than water temperature. All fishermen need to unite to have stringent regulations passed and enforced or we may have very little quality water left for future generations of anglers. This problem is most serious in the northeastern United States and southeast Canada, but is affecting water in areas all over the United States and the rest of the world.

Trout Vision

Much has been written about trout vision and how refraction of light affects the trout's "window." However, I never believed my lack of scientific knowledge in this area hindered my fishing.

I do not believe one can compare what a submerged human can see and make the statement that this is how the trout observe the same thing. I have seen trout on many occasions feeding vigorously on something so minute that I could not see what it was, with my face practically in the water. I have caught many trout at night when it was pitch black on small #18 and #20 flies, so you can see why I am skeptical!

How well and how far a trout can visually detect an angler will always stir up an argument when fishermen get together. I have read and listened to so many theories that I no longer pay them much attention.

On a bright summer day when the water is extremely low and clear and trout are lying in the still, shallow water, they can detect the fishermen at considerable distance. On rare occasions I have spooked trout as far away as fifty to sixty feet. If the sun is in your favor (fishermen between the sun and fish), the same trout may, by a careful, deliberate stalk, be approached as closely as ten to twenty feet. I firmly believe one should approach all trout as closely as possible under existing conditions, whether this be twenty or sixty feet, simply because the fly can be presented much better on a shorter cast. (This will be discussed later.)

Trout can be approached at a much closer distance if one or more of the following conditions are present: an overcast day, slightly discolored water, a deep pool, high water, during rain, or water rippled by the wind. Never fail to take advantage of any natural cover such as high banks, trees, and shrubs. The angler will continue to do better, fishing deliberately and cautiously under any and all conditions.

Angling Sense

How does the neophyte learn where to look for trout when none are showing on the surface? He learns only by experience. The fisherman who began fishing on small mountain or meadow brooks and gradually worked up to larger trout rivers no doubt learned his lessons well. The process takes time but can be speeded up by covering typical water with an experienced angler who will take time to point out the likely spots and explain why trout station themselves at definite places. My advice to the neophyte angler, or anyone who wants to learn where the productive lies are, is to watch for rising trout. In fact, the best procedure to follow the next time you are on a stream during a hatch and see trout showing on the surface, is to take down your rod so that you are not tempted to cast over the rises. Now, observe the rising trout and try to determine why they are feeding at that particular spot and mentally catalog each situation. Cover enough stream so you have a good backlog of all typical feeding positions. Next time you are out, if no trout are rising, fish similar places, skipping all the areas that do not look like the spots you remembered when you were observing the feeding stations. Of course, feeding positions may change during the season.

When trout are feeding on aquatics (such as mayflies) that are hatching in the stream, they will usually feed adjacent to or in the main line of drift.

Trout that live in the very heaviest and fastest water have holding positions on the bottom because of the quieter water there due to boulders and bottom contour. When a heavy hatch is on the surface they may drop down to quieter water or select the less turbulent areas in the rapids to feed. You will learn where these areas are by observation and experience.

In our larger rivers, trout may stay in midstream most of the day and move in close to the banks in the evening and stay there and feed until midmorning. I have seen days on many of our larger trout rivers where one could experience excellent fishing all day along the edges.

I know that the first one to cover any stretch of water should have the most success. After someone covers a stretch of heavily fished water where one must wade, it usually takes several hours for the trout to resume feeding, except during a heavy hatch. On some streams I have fished, trout put down in the morning would be very shy and feed very little until late evening. However, trout are unpredictable and any statement about their behavior and feeding can stir up an interesting debate. Of course, all fly anglers know that the best time to be astream is during a good hatch of aquatic insects, regardless of the time of day.

During the season when terrestrials (grasshoppers, beetles, and ants) are abundant, trout may feed close to the bank where the food is available. That may be in water only a few inches deep. On days with occasional gusty winds, and in areas where there are overhanging trees, I have caught hundreds of trout that were literally gorged with ants. One wonders how so many managed to fall into the water. The same is true when the green inchworms make their appearance. In central Pennsylvania this usually occurs during the last two weeks of May when the oak leaves reach just about one-half their full growth. When trout are feeding on the green worms they become quite selective and at times will not look at a conventional fly.

A good fisherman is alert and sensitive to the changes that take place from hour to hour and day to day throughout the season. These changes are the deciding factors that dictate the lures to use. The trout fishers who do not adapt, or do not have the insight to change to the correct fly patterns, will never reap the satisfaction they should from this grand sport. After all, this is a thinking person's sport.

2
Fishing the Dry Fly

〜〜〜〜〜〜〜

　　　　　　DRY-FLY fishing, in my opinion, is the most fascinating method of taking trout. I suppose this is true because one can see what is going on all the time. The consistently successful angler is one who has acquired the skills necessary to present the fly properly, is thoroughly schooled in the fundamental techniques, and is able to read the water with a fair degree of accuracy.

Fishing the dry fly presents more problems than any other method of angling. For instance, every time the angler lengthens or shortens the line, takes a step up or down or across the stream, a new problem is presented. If he had to take time to make a thorough study of the water before each cast, the dry-fly fisherman would get very little fishing done. This is where experience plays such an important part when it comes to reading the water. The successful and experienced angler presents the fly correctly most of the time. The beginner's first question is "What is the correct presentation?" It varies with almost every cast. When the fly is cast across running water, drag sets in the moment the fly, leader, and line alight, and as the fly drifts with the current it is dragged unnaturally across the surface of the water. Eliminating this drag is the most important fundamental of dry-fly fishing. There is no question in my mind that there is a direct proportion between elimination of drag and the success of the angler. Every person who has ever fished the dry fly has observed trout rising to the imitation, probably following along just inches behind, then refusing the fly and returning to its original station. The inexperienced angler usually surmises he has selected the wrong pattern and proceeds to change to something else. I have seen anglers stand in one spot and change flies for over an hour and still never take a fish. On many occasions, by moving just a step to the right or left the angler could, on the next cast, eliminate drag and take the trout on the original pattern.

I have had the opportunity to fish with many of the best-known fly fishermen in the United States and they all experienced problems with drag. The best of the lot are the ones who are most proficient in mastering the casting techniques that are so necessary to eliminating the unnatural float.

How does one go about eliminating this bugaboo that plagues the dry-fly fisherman? Just by making the presentation in such a manner that fly, leader, and line all alight and float on water that is flowing at the same rate of speed. This is rarely possible. First of all, the fly fisher must learn to cast accurately so he can place the fly exactly where he wants it, and at the same time make the leader and line alight on the water in such a manner (slack line and leader) that the fly has a chance to float as a real insect would over the rising fish. We read a lot about negative and positive curve casts, but as far as I am concerned they have very little value. Once in a while you may be able to use these casts, but all conditions must be perfect. Just one example: If you are fishing with a breeze blowing from left to right, you will make a right-hand curve cast whether you want to or not and it will be impossible to make a negative curve cast! If conditions are suitable the average fly fisher can learn to make the negative and positive curve casts in just a few minutes. All one must do is make a side cast with the rod in the horizontal position. Make a lazy forward cast and just before the line straightens out and the leader and fly are lagging, shoot a little line. The right curve is made from the right side and the left curve cast from the left. With a little practice one can become quite accurate.

Second, approach each rising trout as closely as possible. How close will be determined by such water conditions as clarity, turbidity, speed of current, obstructions, and depth. Remember, the shorter the cast, the better you'll be able to control fly, leader, and line and make them do what you want in order to minimize drag. If possible, maneuver into the best possible position to make the initial cast. Many anglers try to sink the terminal end of the leader. I never worry whether it sinks or not because I don't think it makes any difference as long as you get a drag-free float.

Third is the fly caster's equipment. The most important in eliminating drag is the leader. I have spent more time experimenting with leaders than most other people; this has been a life's hobby and work with me. Probably many will disagree with my design, but my leaders take trout that could not otherwise be taken by me. Most commercial trout leaders are designed to straighten out when they are cast. They have exceptionally heavy butts with quick tapers and are excellent for any kind of fishing where one is not concerned with drag. The mediocre caster would find the leader I use a little harder to cast, but this is the whole secret of its design.

Leader Construction

I am going to relate how this leader adjustment all started. When I was younger I was sure there was a direct relationship between the tippet size and the number of trout I could take. In the mid-thirties when I was teaching at Pennsylvania's Fisherman's Paradise, I was using silkworm gut down to 8X. The reason I caught trout almost at will was because it was practically impossible to straighten out the silkworm gut this fine when it was well soaked. I never gave it a thought that this was giving me a drag-free float.

It is surprising how many dry-fly men really don't recognize drag. I have fished with many who thought they were getting a good float when most of the time there was a noticeable drag. The reason for this in most cases is a straight leader. I have heard some say that they want the leader straight and that they eliminate drag by casting S curves or slack in the line. My experience has taught me that you can have all the S curves you can cast into the line but if the leader is straight you will have drag almost immediately. The slack must be in the leader. The negative and positive curve casts at times are helpful but the times they can be used is limited. Sometimes, if you can position yourself where you can make a cast so that the fly, leader, and line all alight in water flowing at the same rate of speed, you can get a drag-free float, but this is rare on a free-flowing river or stream.

If you are fishing with one who thinks he is getting good floats and trout are refusing to take, have him stand twenty-five or thirty feet from you in a quiet glide and cast a dry fly to his feet on a straight leader and let him observe the drag. Or change places with him, then you tell him if he has drag. He will soon learn why trout have been ignoring his fly so often.

When nylon leaders first came on the market they were heralded as the answer to the fly fisher's prayer. The nylon was stronger than gut in the same sizes and the length could be as long as one wished. Diamond drawn gut over twenty inches was rare.

Back in the thirties and even today most experts recommend leaders with heavy butts, a leader one could cast and straighten out. I believed and tied leaders that way. They are great for streamers and saltwater fly fishing, or for any type of fishing where one is not concerned with surface drag. Even though I tapered the leaders the same as the gut leaders I used they did not perform as well and I could not take as many trout on them. As a result I went back to using gut leaders because the nylon was just too stiff.

Soon the soft nylon followed and I began to experiment, constructing new leaders. I tried leaders tied exclusively with soft nylon. They worked much better than those tied with hard nylon but were not satisfactory for me. It was difficult to cast these leaders back under overhanging trees and they were extremely difficult to cast on windy days. My next try was a basic leader of hard nylon and the tippets of soft nylon. They were far superior to the other two since I knew the elimination of drag was the most important fundamental in dry-fly fishing. The number of fish one can take is in direct proportion to his ability to eliminate drag. Knowing this, I tried another experiment.

Japanese beetles were very abundant in Centre County, Pennsylvania, at the time and I collected a jarful. I made my way to the head of a flat pool I knew held a good population of trout. I sat down on the bank and started a chum line of beetles. It wasn't long until I had about a dozen trout taking every beetle that floated down. Now I took twenty-inch pieces of hard nylon of all the sizes I had with me and inserted the end of the nylon into some of the beetles and sent them down the chum line. Since there was no drag on the nylon the browns picked off most all of the beetles that were attached to the nylon.

This was not my idea. I had read of a similar experiment conducted by John Crowe and I wanted to check it for myself. Let me tell you, I was really impressed. Most of what we read today and what most fly fishermen believe is that the fine terminal part of the leader is more invisible and that this is the reason for using fine tippets. In fact many articles have been written that recommend that the size of the terminal tippet should be determined by the size of the fly one is using. This experiment blasts that theory because the stream-bred browns did not refuse a live beetle on free-floating and drag-free twenty-inch pieces of nylon in sizes up to .015.

I surmised that if I could build a leader that would allow the fly to float drag-free over a rising trout, I could not only take more trout but also use heavier leaders allowing me to release the trout much quicker. This is strictly a conservation measure. The angler who must use 6X, 7X, and 8X terminal tippets to take trout doesn't really play the fish. He applies so little pressure that he actually worries the trout into submission, and when trout are played until they are totally exhausted, many do not survive. I discussed this mortality with Dr. Robert L. Butler, former unit leader of the Cooperative Fisheries Unit, Pennsylvania State University. Briefly, this is what takes place. "Recent work has shown that handling salmonids causes an increase in catecholamines, principally adrenaline. Struggling and hypoxia also results in increase of plastic corticosteroids. The secondary effect of these endocrine changes are a pronounced increase in blood glucose. These stresses of short duration are of relatively long effects. The enjoyment of catching a trout should not be in killing it after it is released. After giving the angler a thrilling experience, they deserve a better fate than this." So let's do away with the old adage that it is more sporting to take fish on light tackle. In my judgment the fly fisherman who can take trout on the heavier tapered leaders is much more skilled in presenting the fly than one who must use the very fine tippets.

The leader I now build allows one to use heavier tippets because it takes into consideration the air resistance of the fly being used. In order to do this it is necessary to adjust the soft nylon or terminal end to accommodate the fly. You cannot build or purchase a leader that will work with all sizes of dry flies without making adjustments. If all dry flies were tied with the same amount of hackle and had the same air resistance, one could build a leader for each size fly, but this is not practical. As an example, a #16 fly, heavily hackled, will react differently than a #16 sparsely tied. The same holds true with all sizes of dry flies. This is why leaders should be checked every time you change a fly. This may be necessary several times a day. If you change flies quite often the tippet will become short and must be replaced and readjusted. When you add the soft nylon as described it is wise to leave the terminal tippet longer than you think necessary.

When you check the leader to see if it is giving you the gradually increasing S curves, this is the procedure to follow. Apply a little more power than you normally need to make a straight cast. Aim the cast about three or four feet above the water where you want the fly to settle. As the line straightens out on the forward cast, check abruptly, then lower the rod and allow the fly to settle on the water. If the terminal tippet is too long the leader will pile up, if too short it will be relatively straight. When it alights with a series of S curves it is adjusted correctly. This is what you need to get a drag-free float.

I start with a small piece of hard nylon (about ten inches) tied to the line with a nail knot. This makes a smoother juncture between the line and leader. I don't count this as part of the leader. My basic leaders are tied with twenty-inch sections of hard nylon in the following sizes: .015, .013, .011, and .009. A supply of these basic leaders are carried at all times and are then adjusted with soft nylon as dictated by the size of the fly I am using.

The following lengths of soft nylon are just approximate because the air resistance and size of the fly being used determine the actual length. When I taper to .007 (4X), I cut off the .009 hard nylon and add soft nylon in the following lengths: 12 inches to 15 inches of .009 (2X), 18 inches of .008 (3X), and 22 inches to 28 inches of .007 (4X). This gives me a leader of approximately 9½ feet.

When I go to .006 (5X), I cut off about half of the .009 (2X) hard nylon and add 12 inches to 15 inches of .008 (3X), 18 inches of .007 (4X), and 22 inches to 30 inches of .006 (5X). This leader will be approximately 10½ feet. If you want to shorten the leader, take several inches off the .015, .013, and .011. I have been using this leader formula for over thirty years and rarely use tippets smaller than .006 (5X) and most of the time I can take trout on leaders tapered to .008 (3X) or .007 (4X).

My friends and I who use this formula have fished all over the Northeast, East, Midwest, and rivers and spring creeks of Wyoming, Montana, and Idaho, and have taken trout on the supposedly tough waters when other fishermen were having difficulty.

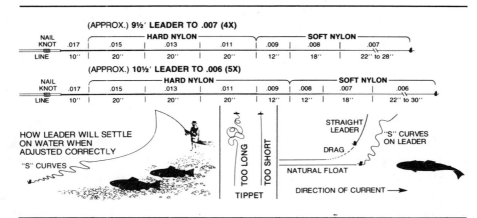

Length of the soft nylon terminal is determined by the air resistance of the dry fly you are using. Leader length and tippet size is NOT determined by the hook size.

Every fly fisherman I have ever demonstrated this leader design to has become an instant convert. I have demonstrated this design to many of the best and most successful angling writers and editors and all are convinced it is the answer for the dry-fly fisherman!

I have been asked by many why I do not use the heavy-butt leaders. My answer is this: I want the S curves in the leader to progressively get longer from the fly to the line. The heavy-butt leaders will not give you this progression. Some contend that a heavy-butt leader is necessary on windy days but I assure you this leader will work under all weather conditions. If you enjoy catching fish rather than casting, this leader is the answer.

Many dry-fly fishermen are concerned with having the leader sink and believe this is important, especially when fishing smooth glides or quiet, slow-moving pools. There are quite a few products on the market today to rub on leaders to sink them. Before using this new design, I must admit I used the leader sink myself. Now I never give it a thought and don't care whether the leader sinks or floats as long as I get a drag-free float.

With over seventy years in fly fishing, there is little concerning the sport about which I would make a definite statement, but this I will: If you use this design for your dry-fly fishing you will increase your catch by at least fifty percent. Some who are now using this formula say it has increased their catch and enjoyment by at least ninety percent. If you don't believe, try it—you will be convinced!

Hatches

Many books have been written on the various hatches of flies important to fly fishermen. Most have merit but for the average angler I suggest the following. Always keep a record of the date, time of day, average size, and color description of hatches you see on streams you most frequently fish. Once you have a record of the hatches you will find they occur at approximately the same time year after year. If you tie your own flies you can duplicate each hatch to your own satisfaction. If not, you can purchase commercial patterns that closely match the natural. I always carry flies that match the local hatches. In addition, I carry other patterns that are proven fish-takers.

There are so many different species of aquatics and terrestrials that have been imitated that one could never carry enough if he wanted to match them all. It is a good thing that a few flies will in most cases take trout from any stream in the world.

Almost every fly fisherman has his own favorite patterns and I firmly believe that confidence in the fly you are using is equally as important as matching the hatch. Flies that are close to the size and color will usually produce if presented properly. However, at times trout can be very selective and then one must have a pattern that closely matches the natural. If I were restricted to seven dry flies I would choose the following in sizes #10 to #20: Adams, Deerhair Ant, Light Cahill, Gordon Quill, Sulphur, Spruce Creek, and Trico (dun and spinner). Of course one should have a selection of wet flies, nymphs, and streamer types and use them when necessary.

Shortly after I started the angling course at Pennsylvania State University, I thought I should include a lecture or two on the identification of the major hatches. I finally decided it was not necessary. I had cards printed with the names of the most common hatches in Pennsylvania, the date and time of day emergence normally occurred, and distributed them to the students. If one follows the preceding suggestions it is not necessary to take the time to learn all the scientific names. I would rather spend my time experimenting with new techniques and fishing!

Responding to the Rise

When trout are showing on the surface (splash-rising, dimpling, bulging), the angler should determine if the trout are actually feeding on the duns or spinners or if they are taking the nymphs just below the surface, in the surface film, or on the surface. If the naturals are large enough to see, watch one individual fly at a time; follow it until you can be sure it is being taken on the surface. Only by careful observation can you be sure which type of imitation should be presented.

The accepted practice is to fish the dry fly upstream. In my opinion this is the most enjoyable and practical way to fish and gives the angler a better perspective of everything that is happening. When trout are surface-feeding you can follow the line of drift and have a better chance to read the water before making the initial cast. This of course helps determine just how to present the fly in order to eliminate drag. There are certain procedures I follow when casting to trout in various types of water. In fast-moving, riffly water, the fly is presented above and as close to the rise as possible. When trout are feeding close to cover such as grassy undercut banks, alongside boulders, logs, or debris, one must try to cast so that the fly almost brushes the cover as it floats by.

It is seldom you will find a large trout surface-feeding on our heavily fished eastern waters. When you are lucky enough to find one, extreme care must be taken in your presentation if you are to be successful. This is where skill and knowledge pay off.

When fishing a hackled dry fly in relatively quiet, slow-moving water, I like to present the fly on a slack leader as previously described so the fly will float directly over the feeding trout without drag. I prefer to be stationed a little off to one side as shown in the illustration.

Presenting a terrestrial is at times quite different. In riffly water the terrestrials are presented the same as the hackled dry fly. On relatively quiet water and smooth water off the main stem of the current I put additional power in the cast and actually plop the ant, cricket, or grasshopper on the water. This disturbance will attract trout from a considerable distance. It is not unusual for a trout to rush to the imitation from as far away as ten or fifteen feet. Remember, when you are fishing over a rising fish your chances of taking it become less and less with each succeeding cast. Try to make your first cast as near perfect as possible. If you do make a bad cast, don't rip the line and fly from the water, let it float away from the fish and wait until it rises once or twice before trying again. You must be patient if you want to reap the fullest enjoyment with the dry fly.

Of course, you are going to get into situations where you are forced to fish the dry fly across stream, and at times downstream. Sometimes a fly dragged across the surface in short jerks will excite the trout into striking. This is especially true during a caddisfly hatch and with spiders and Variants. At this time twitching and jerking the fly will often be better than a natural drift.

On meadow streams where sedges, grass, and weeds grow right to the water's edge and trout are feeding close to the banks, one of the most deadly methods of taking a trout is by dapping. The longer rods are better for this type of fishing; a heavy leader may be used. With line and leader about the length of the rod, crawl up to the bank, extend the rod out over the stream, and dap (or touch) the fly on the surface. Years ago, on Spring Creek in Pennsylvania, I used to take many large trout using this method on the long, smooth meadow pools. Actually no skill is involved in dapping a fly. Success amounts to concealment. I would not think of trying to fish this way again.

In most cases when trout rise and take a dry fly, one should strike immediately. The length of the cast or the distance the fly is from the angler when the strike occurs determines the rod position. When a strike occurs fifty feet or so from the angler, the position of the rod should be about horizontal with the water. As the fly drifts toward the angler, the rod should be gradually elevated. In other words, have the rod in a position so that you strike against the spring of the rod. When I find a large trout feeding in relatively quiet water, I try to be quite deliberate and allow the trout to start to settle before striking. The same holds true with all sizes of trout when using flies #18 and smaller.

There is no question in my mind that in most cases the easiest way to fish a dry fly is downstream. It has this advantage: you can usually use heavier terminal tackle, thus giving you an advantage on large trout. In many instances it is easier to eliminate drag. On rare occasions I will deliberately fish the dry fly downstream, but it just doesn't seem right to take the easy route. I love the challenge of fishing the dry fly using the conventional methods, and I believe most dry-fly fishermen feel the same way.

3

Tricorythodes:
The Most Important Hatch

BECAUSE most trout seasons have been extended until fall, and in some cases year round, in the United States, the Trico has become an important hatch for the dedicated trout angler. This is true because most of these hatches are of long duration and are predictable. One who can consistently take trout on this tiny mayfly will have no difficulty taking trout on any other pattern.

I saw my first Trico spinner fall in late July 1927 on my third trip to Pennsylvania's famous Spring Creek. Ab Larson and I camped next to Benner Spring where there was a long pool below the confluence of the spring and the main stream. About eight o'clock the next morning trout began to rise all over the pool. I had never seen this many trout rising in one pool in all my previous experience. We hurriedly assembled our tackle and started fishing with the flies we normally used for brook trout on Northern Tier mountain streams. Eventually I noticed tiny mayflies in the air and in a back eddy and realized this was what the trout were feeding on. The smallest flies we had were #16 and they were worthless. It was humbling to see hundreds of trout rising and not be able to catch a single one.

I next fished this hatch in July 1934 when I worked at Pennsylvania's Fisherman's Paradise on Spring Creek, a few miles upstream from Bellefonte, Pennsylvania. One morning in mid-July Charlie Mench, a member of the Pennsylvania Fish Commission, came to the booth where I was teaching fly tying and asked me to tie him a small black fly. I tied him a black quill on the smallest hook I had, a #20. He walked in back of the booth and immediately caught a beautiful brown over twenty inches long. Needless to say, it didn't take me long to tie some for myself, and the next morning I caught my first trout on a Trico. Sometime later I noticed the dun had a greenish body and I tied a blue dun hackled fly with a greenish body and fished it along with the blue quill and used these two patterns until I started using the hackleless spinner flies with black and olive-green dubbed bodies in about 1977.

I am quite sure the Horse Collar Nymph, when fished during the hatch, is taken for the Trico nymph. The best two patterns for me were the ones with blackish and greenish bodies.

Recently I have experimented with various small nymphs and found the Horse Collar worked well during the hatch. However, the greenish olive dubbed is my favorite because it is more buoyant and can be fished near or on the surface—the most productive method for me. None of my acquaintances knew what the fly was and Ray Bergman, the trout-fishing great and outdoor writer who fished the Paradise for several days that July, called the fly a midge. So did I, until 1961 when the late Bill Pfeiffer had the fly identified probably as *Tricorythodes atratus* by Dr. B. A. Burks of Illinois. As I look back over the years I have many fond memories of the hatch.

In early September 1935, Pennsylvania State University offered me the position of starting a physical education program at the Forestry School at Mont Alto, Pennsylvania. The first day there I met Bill Pfeiffer, an ardent fly fisherman. Of course it wasn't long until we started talking about fishing and Bill told me about the great hatch of small flies on the now famous Falling Spring Creek, about seven miles from the campus. At that time the Pennsylvania trout season closed the end of July, but the hatch was still coming off the stream. Bill drove me over the next morning to show me Falling Spring Creek and I saw the greatest hatch I had ever witnessed. We stopped at several accesses to the stream and watched the trout feeding on the small flies. There were so many rising trout I could hardly believe my eyes and almost all the trout were stream-bred rainbows! Bill told me the hatch usually started around the last of June, which was earlier than on Spring Creek.

Until 1940 I only had a chance to fish the hatch on Falling Spring Creek a few times because I was working at the Paradise and on brook-trout research on the Kettle Creek watershed in Potter County, Pennsylvania, with R. L. Watts, dean of the College of Agriculture at Pennsylvania State University. From that date on I have spent every available hour fishing this hatch.

During the 1940–41 and 1942 seasons I fished almost every morning on Falling Spring Creek and only saw two other fishermen fly-fishing the stream. At that time you could only fish short stretches of water because there were so many rises and one could catch a trout on almost every cast. Most of the trout were under a foot long, but fish to eighteen inches were quite common.

Although I have fished the Trico hatches on streams in Idaho, Michigan, Montana, New York, Pennsylvania, and Vermont, most of my fishing has been done in Pennsylvania. I have read there are fourteen Trico species identified in North America and more may be classified in the future. I must admit I can only be sure of *Tricorythodes atratus* and do not know the species I have fished on other streams.

I have spent thousands of hours astream fishing the hatch. Since the spinner fall usually only lasts about two hours, this represents quite a number of days! When the trout season was extended in Pennsylvania to Labor Day in 1956, the hatch started to become popular. Then, in 1979, the season was extended on all streams but those classified as Wild Trout Streams from the opening of the season until March first. This allowed one to fish the hatch until it ended with the first heavy frost, usually the last of October or early November.

In 1987 I decided to make a study of the Trico hatch on Spruce Creek in Pennsylvania to try to clear up some of the things I was not sure of. I spent many hours observing the flies from dawn until the hatch was over, and in addition I had help from two friends who are trained biologists. One was Dr. Robert Carline, leader of the Pennsylvania State Cooperative Fish and Wildlife Research Unit, who loaned me a doctoral dissertation by Dr. Ronald J. Hall. (*Life History: Drift and Production Rate of the Stream Mayfly* Tricorythodes atratus *(Mc donnough) in the Headwaters of the Mississippi River.* University of Minnesota, 1975.) In addition, he discussed with me what he knew about the hatch. The other was Charlie Meck, who retired from Pennsylvania State University to devote his time to writing and entomology. He is a trained biologist, avid fly fisherman, and outdoor writer whose book *Meeting and Fishing the Hatches* covers major hatches over most of the United States. Charlie graciously spent time with me on Spruce Creek and we observed together all that takes place during the hatch. He definitely identified the Trico species *atratus*. We collected the female nymphs and observed the duns emerge and fly up into the tops of the trees bordering the stream. The only blackish male duns we saw were caught on cobwebs in the grass along the stream bank after they emerged at night.

The study Dr. Carline gave me to review cleared up a puzzle that had baffled me for years. I arrived at the stream dozens of times at daybreak and watched the duns hatch, but when the spinners appeared there were thousands more than I saw emerge. Here is the answer: The male duns, blackish in color, start emerging just after dusk and continue until just before dawn and apparently fly to the trees bordering the stream. They evidently fly high up in the trees because I have never observed any low enough for me to see them. While in the trees they molt into spinners.

The female duns emerge just before dawn and continue usually until nine or ten o'clock. During the latter part of the season (September and October) on cooler mornings I have observed a few emerging as late as noon. The female emerges from the greenish nymph and her abdomen is greenish in color due to the eggs it is packed with.

When the nuptial flight takes place the males start first and the females join them. The males seem to stay on top of the swarms. I am reasonably sure they do so when they get down close to the riffly areas. Once John Randolph, editor of *Fly Fisherman* magazine, and I were checking a swarm and all the Tricos John caught in the net, five or six feet above the water, were females—the ones on top were males.

When the female oviposits the small greenish ball that may contain up to four hundred eggs, her abdomen becomes a whitish color. I have found that when the spinner fall starts, all the flies floating on the water are females. It is rare to see a blackish male spinner at this time. Toward the end of the hatch you will see a few males, but not in great numbers. However, at the end of the spinner fall when only a few flies are on the water, they are all males.

A good example follows: On August 31 at eight in the morning, with air temperatures at sixty degrees, female spinners oviposited and were floating on the surface of the water. On September 1 at eight o'clock, with air temperatures at fifty-four degrees, spinners were not on the water until nine-fifteen. In both cases the hatch was over in approximately two hours and only a few males were seen. This is characteristic of the hatch—the cooler the morning the later the hatch. Even on cloudy mornings the hatch appeared later.

The *atratus* species is a two-generation mayfly. After the eggs are deposited, the second generation emerges forty-nine days later. This continues every day from the start of the hatch until the first heavy frost, and then they are diapause until the next July when it starts all over. I never observed a great decrease in the number of spinners from the beginning to the end of the hatch during the approximately three and one-half to four months it occurs on Spruce and Spring Creeks.

Another observation I think is important and has never been published is that in heavily shaded areas of the streams the hatch is very sparse or nonexistent. It appears to need sunlight.

Fishing the Hatch

I don't know of any competent fly fisherman who does not enjoy the challenge of this hatch. The casual fly angler who is not interested in improving his knowledge of the sport will never do well with the Trico. However, serious anglers are devoted to the hatch because it offers some of the most gratifying angling of the whole season. The fly fishermen of my acquaintance who pursue the Trico are the most skilled anglers I know.

In my experience, when trout start feeding on a good hatch they become very selective and if the presentation is not near perfect they will ignore the artificial. If there is any drag they will rarely take. If you are using a good imitation and the trout are refusing your presentation I suggest you turn back to the section on leader construction and see if your leader design is correct. You should be able to learn how to build your leader and then cast to get the S-curve effect in a very short time. When you have it down pat you will be surprised how easy it is and how many trout you are able to catch. You do not need to strike quickly. If you do you will miss many. Just raise the rod tip enough to tighten the line and you will hook many more trout.

Equally important is your approach to rising trout. You must approach a fish in low, clear water carefully, especially if the water is also smooth. Trout can be spooked, depending on water conditions, much more than you would suspect. This is true in the latter part of the season on heavily fished streams, and especially on clear sunny days. When I walk down a stream to fish a stretch of water, I keep at least thirty to forty feet away from the bank or the rising trout. If I must walk closer than this, I slow down and don't make any sudden movements. When I reach the pool or run where I intend to start fishing, I approach the casting position as slowly as possible. How slow is this? I always suggest walking as slowly as possible, then cutting that pace to half speed. If I must wade, I follow the same procedure so I don't push waves ahead of me and spook the fish. I have seen trout stop feeding the moment a wave disturbs the surface. Careless wading is the most common error an angler can make when fishing this or any other hatch. Of course, in riffly water one can approach much closer to any rising trout. I like to keep the sun at my back whenever possible. This permits me to approach much closer.

It is quite common during the Trico hatch to find a pod of six to twelve trout rising within casting distance. If you want to catch as many as possible, you must cast from below to the closest fish first. Then, if you hook this fish, try to keep it from running to the fish above. If you can do this and release the fish without too much disturbance, it is possible to catch the majority of the rising fish. With the strong tippet material we have today you can control the average trout. One should use barbless hooks when using small artificials because they are easier to extract. With a hemostat, a barbless hook can easily be removed even when it has been taken deep in the mouth or throat.

Casting Tactics

There is no doubt the best casting position is below and a little to the side of the rise, so you can cast the line, leader, and fly in water that is flowing at a single rate of speed. The cast should be made so the fly alights six to twelve inches above the rise, and the leader kept from floating over the rise if possible. At times the fish is in such a position that you must have the leader pass over the fish, and if the cast is delicate enough, a high percentage of trout will take. There are many times when this approach is not possible, however. The greater the angle you must cast to a rise, the closer you should try to present the fly. Although it is not possible under many stream situations, particularly on breezy or windy days, I try to have the fly alight just a few inches above the rise; of course, the longer the float, the more chance drag will start before the fly passes over the fish.

There are some situations where it is impossible to make the cast so that you will get the S curves in the leader. The most common are when the wind is blowing upstream or across and when you must cast under branches and obstructions. When one must fish under these conditions, all you can do is your best. Many anglers prefer to make the downstream cast, especially when fishing larger rivers or where the situation will not allow for an upstream cast.

When I must cast downstream, I like to approach the fish as closely as possible. When I determine how much line I need to reach the fish, I strip off additional yards. Now I make a slack-leader cast, and when it lands on the water I feed the additional line. If the presentation is re-fused, I slowly move the rod as far as possible to the left or right so that the line gradually moves away from the rise, then I retrieve the line slowly before making another cast.

Trico Information

When one should start fishing the hatch is a decision of individual pref-erence. If you are on the stream at daybreak and the fish are working on the duns and nymphs, you may fish for the rising fish. You can continue fishing them until the spinners start to fall. When fishing the duns, I seem to do a little better with a sparsely tied hackle fly with white or light blue dun wings, olive-green body, and light blue dun hackle. How-ever, the no-hackle spinner flies will take trout at this time. In fact, when the duns are hatching, you can usually have good action on the nymph. At times I have caught as many or more on the nymph.

I usually don't fish the hatch when the duns are hatching but wait for the spinner fall because most of the fish in a given pool are then working and feeding voraciously. I just don't like to disturb a pool or area before the best time of the hatch occurs.

How many trout one can catch during a normal spinner fall depends on several factors: the stream must support a good number of fish and the angler must be skillful enough to be able to make a slack-leader cast to avoid drag.

I have helped many anglers with this problem and those who paid attention usually could catch trout at once. I will relate one of the best examples. A few years ago Rosalynn Carter asked me to work with her before the spinner fall. I demonstrated the casting technique and in a few minutes she had it down pat. As soon as the spinners settled on the water she began to take trout. I stood beside her and netted and released twenty-one trout she had caught without moving from the original position. I should add she is the fastest learner I have ever instructed because she concentrates on what she is doing. She could have taken many more trout from the same position but called her son, Chip, to come and take her place, and he caught a few.

One of the best Trico anglers I know, and one of my best friends, is Dr. Ralph Dougherty. We have observed and fished the hatch many times over the years. It is not uncommon for us to straighten out the bend or break the hook off and just see how many trout we can raise. This way we never have to play or release the hooked trout. After all, presenting the fly so the trout will take is the most important part of dry-fly fishing.

The New Trico Flies

Last season I saw Krystal Flash material at the Fly Fisherman's Paradise Tackle Shop. Since I have trouble seeing small flies, I purchased some Krystal Flash and tied spinners, using this material for wings. The resulting spinner was not only easier to see, but the wings did not mat up like the poly material I formerly used. Because it was so much easier to see, I began to take more trout.

One September day, while sitting on a bench along Spruce Creek with Lefty Kreh waiting for the spinner fall to begin, I showed him some of the new flies and gave him a few. He adjusted his leader and as soon as the spinners settled on the water we went down to a pool that I knew held a good pod of trout. Lefty moved into position and on the first cast connected with a beautiful native brown. He remained in that position and proceeded to land a half-dozen more trout. Lefty was really excited about the material for spinner wings because he could see it fifty feet away. I am sure by now he has tied up enough to last him for years.

The next morning I guided Bill Anderson, another excellent Trico angler, to some of the best pools. Lefty told him about the new winged spinners and I gave Bill a few of the flies. He, too, caught many trout on this fly pattern and, like Lefty, he agreed it was much easier to see and the wings held their form better than poly wings. I now tie a spinner with a creamy white body to represent the female after the eggs are dropped. I believe it works a little better than the ones I tie with the olive-green and black bodies.

On most streams I prefer a nine-foot rod that handles a 3- or 4-weight line with enough backbone to allow me to have a good check. On the larger western rivers I have fished, I use a ten-foot rod that will handle a 4- or 5-weight line. The leaders I use are usually from nine and a half to ten and a half feet. Accuracy is more difficult with the longer leader. If you learn how to make the check cast, longer leaders are not necessary.

The flies I now use are tied on the new Tiemco Trico hooks, sizes #20 and #22. I prefer the Tiemco hooks for all my personal flies and all Trico patterns because they are short-shanked, sharp-pointed, and have the smallest barb of any hook on the market. I used to use hooks as small as #28 but the gap on the #20 and #22 hooks is much better than the smaller sizes. Some Trico species may require a smaller hook, and if so, use them.

I use these Tiemco hooks for all my Trico patterns: #500 U in #20 and #22—this is a short-shanked hook with a turned-up eye and is available in #16 to #22; and #501 in #20 and #22—this is a short-shanked hook with a ringed eye and is available in #20 to #28.

Trico Patterns

Female Nymph

TAIL:	A few blue dun hackles
BODY:	Olive-green dubbing
LEGS:	One wind of blue dun hackle, trimmed at top and bottom
WING PAD:	Small build-up with dubbing

Female Dun

TAIL:	A few blue dun barbules
BODY:	Olive-green dubbing
WINGS:	Light blue dun or white hackle tips
HACKLES:	Light blue dun

Spinners

#1	TAIL:	Black hackle barbules
	BODY:	Black dubbing
	WINGS:	Pearl Krystal Flash
#2	TAIL:	Blue dun barbules
	BODY:	Abdomen olive-green dubbing, thorax black dubbing
	WINGS:	Pearl Krystal Flash
#3	TAIL:	Blue dun barbules
	BODY:	Abdomen creamy white, thorax black dubbing
	WINGS:	Pearl Krystal Flash

MALE SPINNER

FEMALE NYMPH

FEMALE DUN

FEMALE SPINNER

4

Wet-Fly Fishing

~~~~~~~~~~~

WHEN one fishes with any artificial fly that sinks below the surface film it should be called wet-fly fishing. Included are the common wet fly, nymph, bucktail, and streamer. Every method or technique used to fish any one of the above creations can be used on the other. Many fishermen have the impression that all one has to do to fish the wet fly is to cast out in the current, allow the fly to drift downstream, impart a little action, and when it reaches the end of the float, retrieve back with short jerks. Nothing could be further from the truth. There are so many methods and techniques of fishing the wet fly that whole books have been devoted to this one subject. The wet fly, depending on conditions, is fished from the surface film to the stream bottom in riffly, smooth glides or quiet water, upstream or down. Conditions change so rapidly on any one stream that to be successful the angler may have to change methods a dozen or more times a day.

In my opinion, when fishing the wet fly downstream, the most important fundamental is to keep the line and leader as straight as possible between the rod tip and fly. At the same time, the angle between the line and the rod tip should be no more than approximately ninety degrees. Anyone who can manipulate the rod and line to achieve this most of the time during the float cannot fail to take trout with the wet fly. Let us see why this is so important. When a cast is made down and across any stream, drag immediately sets in. When there is a belly in the line and leader, it is usually difficult to tell when one has a strike. In addition, it is more difficult to hook the fish.

Let us take a typical situation with a right-handed person fishing downstream from the left bank. The cast is made almost perpendicularly across the stream, with the fastest current in the center. As soon as the fly, leader, and line alight, the line in the fastest water is bellied out downstream and causes the fly to swing around and follow the line. If the cast is not too long, by manipulating the rod to the left (from its position at the completion of the cast) and keeping it horizontal to the water, it is possible to keep the line relatively straight from the rod tip at ninety degrees or less. When you can no longer keep the line straight from the rod tip to the fly by following this procedure, you must "mend" the line to straighten out the belly. This is done by raising the rod tip almost to the vertical and by bringing it sharply down and to the right upstream. That will throw the belly from the downstream to an upstream position. The mending process must be done with just enough force to move the line but not flip the fly or cast of flies out of the water. This can only be done when fishing with a relatively long line; it is difficult to mend a short line.

Why is this so important? If you keep the angle between the line and the rod tip ninety degrees or less, when you get a strike the fish will be striking against the spring of the rod. When the rod tip is pointed at the fly in a horizontal position, many fish will tear off as soon as they hit the fly. I am sure every wet-fly fisherman has had the experience of feeling a heavy strike and knowing the fish has been hooked, only to have it tear loose. The usual alibi is that the trout are hitting short, but if you follow the preceding advice you will land a high percentage of the fish you formerly lost. Of course, it stands to reason that the straighter the line between the rod tip and the fly, the more trout will be hooked. In fact, most trout in such situations will hook themselves or can easily be hooked by just raising the rod tip.

The volume and size of the stream you are fishing and how deep the fish are taking determines whether you should use a floating or sink-tip line. I prefer to use the floating line whenever possible and many times use it when I know a sinking line would do a better job.

The most popular way to fish the wet fly is by the natural-drift method. Here the angler casts across, or down and across, the stream and allows the fly to drift naturally in the current. The line may be mended to keep it straight and additional line may be released to give a longer drift. When the drift is terminated and starts to drag across the stream you should be on the lookout for a strike. This is the point where the fly has the most action, is moving faster, and starts rising to the surface. Trout may have followed the fly some distance and will probably strike at this point because of the increased action.

If the fly is still in what looks like good holding water, one may retrieve the fly by hand twists or by stripping in line, at the same time giving a little action by twitching the rod tip.

The wet-fly fisherman can follow the same procedure, giving the fly a little action throughout the entire float by occasionally or rhythmically twitching the rod tip. Sometimes a little action will excite trout into striking when the natural drift is unproductive.

Usually when I know I am going to be fishing downstream I rig up a cast of two or three wet flies. The size of the stream I am fishing determines the distance between the flies. On average eastern waters the flies should be about twenty inches apart, on large rivers about twenty-four to thirty inches. In tying up a wet-fly leader I usually leave the heaviest section of the blood knot sticking out about five inches. To this I attach the wet fly. I have always had better success if I kept the distance from the fly to the leader short, usually from two to two and a half inches. Longer droppers are always getting wrapped around the leader or knotted and do not fish as they should.

Many times in fast, riffly water where there are many pockets and rocks, you can fish a short line and excite trout into striking by playing the flies over the pockets, around the rocks, holding them still a few minutes then twitching the rod tip, or jerking the flies along six or eight inches at a time. The hand fly, or the one nearest the line, should always be just dapping the water. On occasion this fly will take more trout than the other two.

When I am fishing three flies I usually start out with a black fly on the end, the middle fly a ginger or brown, and the hand fly a gray or blue dun. If one fly seems to be producing better than the others I may change so I have two or sometimes three of the same flies on the cast. At times I will use a weighted nymph on the end and two wet flies on the droppers.

On quiet, still water one generally must impart some action to the flies. No one can predict what action is best. It is a rare occasion when all the various methods and actions are tried that at least some trout cannot be taken.

When fishing the wet fly upstream I generally use one fly and pay the same attention to drag as when fishing the dry fly. Since the fly is under the surface it is not always possible to see the trout strike. When unable to see the fish strike I watch the line and strike when it stops or gives a little jerk. One reason I prefer a white or light-colored line is because I can see it so much better. This is especially true when fishing shady stretches of water or just at dusk.

Here again you may have to impart some action to the fly if the natural drift does not work. When trout are not taking, try every kind of action you can think of. In addition, you may have to fish at varying depths (as will be discussed in the section on nymph fishing). After all, the wet-fly fisherman who uses only one method is going to go fishless many more times than the fisherman who is versatile and changes methods, retrieves, depth, and flies as dictated by conditions.

Nymph Fishing

Nymphing is a term for one method of wet-fly fishing. Usually the creations tied to imitate the nymphal stage of the various aquatic insects look a little more like the natural than does the wet fly. Many imitations are so perfect that at arm's length they are difficult to tell from the natural.

I have been fishing the nymph since 1929 and believe if I were restricted to only one artificial lure to fish for trout throughout the season the choice would have to be a nymph. My reason is simple: The bulk of the food that trout feed on day in and day out during the year is subsurface in nature. This includes the nymphs or larvae of all aquatic insects as well as scuds and freshwater shrimp. In addition, the nymph can be fished successfully in all types of water from small mountain or meadow brooks to large rivers. Whether the water is high and discolored or low and crystal clear seems to make little difference. Trout, if they are feeding at all, will rarely refuse a nymph if it is presented right.

In 1934 I was hired by the Pennsylvania Fish Commission to teach fly tying and casting at Fisherman's Paradise, located near Bellefonte on the then famous Spring Creek. At that time the stream harbored more large trout than any stream I have ever fished. Most fishermen knew very little about nymph fishing and on this water I introduced hundreds of fishermen to this "new method" of fishing.

Actually, nymphing had been practiced and used by many Americans before this time, but little was ever put in print, so it was a "new method" for most anglers who fished at the Paradise. At that time most of the fishermen used bucktails, streamers, and large dry or wet flies in sizes #10 to #14. Most fishermen caught trout right after the opening at 8:00 A.M. but after a few hours the fish became quite shy and very few were caught. I could put on a weighted nymph at this time and in the deeper riffles and pools take trout almost at will.

During the time I worked there I caught many thousands of trout that ranged in lengths from about a foot up to over twenty-eight inches. Of course I fished all kinds of artificials (wet, dry, bucktails, and streamers), but the bulk of the large trout were taken on nymphs. Spring Creek in those days held a tremendous population of stream-bred fish, but in the Paradise area, because of angling pressure, trout were stocked nearly every week throughout the open season. After a couple of days of pounding by hundreds of fishermen with all degrees of skill, the stocked trout became quite shy and were just as difficult to take as the native fish. Needless to say, everyone wanted to know what I was using and as a result it wasn't long until the nymph was a common lure at the Paradise.

Although many were fishing in a way they thought of as nymphing, few really understood what they were doing. Some would cut off the wings from a wet fly, leave a little stump, then fish it deep. You were only allowed to use one or two split shot but this was usually sufficient. Nymphing to most was just getting the fly on the bottom and striking every time it stopped. Some were successful and caught a few trout but soon learned that there was a lot they did not know, that there were many ways a nymph can be presented to the trout.

Most of the nymphs I used at that time were weighted with lead wire then dubbed with muskrat, mink, beaver, rabbit, or Australian opossum fur and tied on hooks from #10 to #16. On almost all the nymphs I tied as a youngster, I took a dubbing needle and picked out the fur to give a very rough appearance. Today I tie many versions using all the various synthetics available.

When I first introduced the small midge larva, #18, #20, and #22 at the Paradise in 1934, many doubted they would take large trout. It didn't take long until I sold all I could find time to tie! They were an instant success and I still have fly fishermen writing to me for samples of this creation.

From midsummer to fall when the water is low and clear, these small midge larva will produce most all day long. I fish them from top to bottom and at times they are very effective when fished dry on the surface. They were very difficult for me to see, so on some I tied hackle-tip wings and it helped. I believe this was the beginning of the no-hackle fly. I think I was the first fly tyer in the country to tie the small #18, #20, and #22 midge larva, and I can assure you I would never be without an ample supply.

Charlie Fox, one of the premier fly anglers and fishing writers in the United States, is responsible for the naming of the small creation. During the spring of 1936 I was fishing the dam at the head of the famous Big Spring at Newville, Pennsylvania. I waded out in the dam so I could reach the main channel, tied on an all-black midge larva and caught brook trout on almost every cast. After a half hour of this fantastic fishing I walked down to the Old Mill and there met Charlie. He wanted to know what I was using and I told him it was the same midge larva I had been using at the Paradise. He said "Oh, the Horse Collar Nymph," and the name stuck. In addition, he ordered ten or twelve dozen. Charlie experimented with the various color combinations and eventually he preferred the olive-green.

In his book *Rising Trout,* Charlie wrote about his success with this midge nymph. It is very simple to tie: a few small barbs for the tail, dubbed silk or quill body, and two turns of the finest chenille for the head (see Diagram 45). You can also build up a head with tightly spun dubbing.

This small nymph is not always a producer but is so good I would never venture on the stream from mid-May on without a generous supply in all colors. They have saved the day for me on many occasions.

The nymphs I use today are many and vary in size from the large #6 and #4 that the great writer and western nympher Charlie Brooks developed, to the small #22. Charlie was a good friend and showed me how to fish these large nymphs in the heavy turbulent riffles. If it hadn't been for him, I would never have enjoyed this type of nymphing; he added a new dimension to my fly angling.

All the methods described for the wet fly may be used for nymph fishing. As a general rule, however, a fast jerk retrieve, as sometimes used with the wet fly, does not seem to work as well with the imitation nymphs. Most nymphs I have observed are usually fast swimmers and when dislodged from under rocks move quite rapidly, except the crawlers. The few I have seen emerging swim rather slowly to the surface with an undulating movement.

At times when the nymphs are shucking their cases and emerging as duns, trout will refuse the dun and feed heavily on the emerging nymphs as they make their way from the streambed to the surface. I have seen them be quite selective on many occasions and take the nymph only when it was floating on the surface. When there are nymphs and duns on the surface one must be quite observant to be sure which phase the trout are taking, especially at the beginning of a hatch. Quite often the trout will switch in just a few minutes and take the duns and refuse the nymphs. To float the nymph, dress it and about six to ten inches of the end of the leader with line-dressing material. I use light-wire hooks in almost all nymphs except those that are weighted to be fished on the bottom. Fishing a nymph as a dry fly is not new. I first wrote about this method in 1937.

Weighted nymphs fished on the bottom take the most big trout. To fish this way you must develop a delicate touch or sense of feeling to be successful. The types of water best suited for this kind of nymphing are heavy riffles, pocket water, and relatively deep pools. The nymph is much easier to fish correctly in water that has a pretty good current.

Pocket water, along the sides of logs or boulders, and along undercut banks are the choice spots as far as I am concerned.

I cannot fish the weighted nymph well on a long line. A long cast for me is approximately thirty feet. In almost all cases I fish the nymph upstream using a floating line. I make the cast upstream and allow the nymph to settle to the bottom. When fishing pocket water, always cast the nymph to the head of the pocket. Make the cast a couple of feet high. As the cast straightens out, check the rod sharply. This will allow the nymph to drop so it will quickly sink before the current starts to pull and drag the line. I call this the tuck cast and it is the most important fundamental one should learn when fishing pocket or riffly water. If the cast is made so the line, leader, and fly are in a straight line, the nymph cannot fish on the bottom as it should. The moment the nymph touches the streambed I raise the rod tip just enough to keep the nymph drifting along as close to the bottom as possible. If there are boulders, logs, or undercut banks where a trout may be bedding, I allow the nymph to float as close to the hiding places as I can without getting hung up. Of course, if the water is slightly off color, one may approach much closer to the suspected lies. It should be noted, however, that trout can be taken by this method even when the water is very low and gin clear. The nice part about deep nymph fishing is that when one becomes proficient, very few trout are missed.

As the nymph is drifting back toward me I watch the end of the line close to the leader. If I see it stop or jerk I immediately strike. Once in a while you will snag debris on the bottom, but when you are fishing correctly and develop a certain sense of knowing what the nymph is doing, snags will be few and far between. If I am fishing up and across the stream, I always keep the rod tip ahead of the drifting line. If the line drifts below the rod tip I cannot tell what the nymph is doing, so I make another cast.

As far as I know, I was the first to introduce this casting technique and the best nymph fishermen I know today use it. One of the first I showed this cast to years ago was my friend Joe Humphreys and he uses it all the time. He has taught it to hundreds in his angling classes. Joe, by the way, is the best nympher of all my acquaintances who like to fish "down under."

Nymph fishing is one of the easiest and most successful methods for the dedicated fly fisherman to learn. Here again, one must continually change tactics according to stream conditions. One method will not work all the time and the most successful are those who can quickly determine at what level the fish are feeding and then present the nymph in such a manner that the trout will take. If you can follow these suggestions I am sure you will be in for some pleasant surprises. The next time you are fishing and having poor luck with all other methods, try nymphing. It may be the making of the day for you.

One researcher, who has spent a lot of time observing trout, states that they feed all the time from April through October. This may be true on a stream where no fishing is permitted, but on all the waters I have fished I have never found this to be true. I have spent many hours fishing with the best fly anglers I know and we have experienced many hours and days when it was just not possible to raise a single fish. I would sure like this researcher to be with me when I run into these blank periods and show me how to induce the trout to take my offering. I have so much to learn!

Nymph fishing is not only imitating the mayflies and stoneflies (incomplete metamorphosis), but also imitating those with complete metamorphosis (egg, larva, pupa, and adult) such as the caddis. With this type of angling one must remember that trout usually feed on the most available food but at times will take anything that looks edible. When you have fast-swimming nymphs and slow crawlers, it is no wonder nymphing can be complicated. Many nymph fishermen use an indicator on the leader to help them see a pick-up or strike.

Cortland Line Company markets a line designed for nymph fishing. The terminal end is dyed a pink fluorescent color and can be seen much better than a normal light-colored line can. I tested this line for several years before it was put on the market and it increases the number of trout I can take when nymph fishing.

Bucktails and Streamers

I do not think there is any doubt in the minds of most fishermen that bucktail and streamer flies probably catch the largest trout for most anglers. Looking at the lures responsible for trout taken in contests or

record trout, bucktails and streamers usually head the list. Most of the flies are tied to represent one of the main sources of trout food, the minnow. Many gaudy patterns are tied and some are quite popular, such as the Mickey Finn. This fly could not possibly represent anything living in the water. I use only a few patterns but have a good range of color and hook size.

Most fishermen are under the impression that these flies are best used during periods when the water is high or discolored, or for early-season work. I have found they are effective all season long and under any and all conditions. All the methods described for the wet fly and nymph may be used with bucktails and streamers, but a sharper and faster retrieve generally works better with these flies. A pretty good rule to follow is: In muddy water fish with a very slow retrieve, as the water gets correspondingly clearer flies may be fished faster. In other words, the clearer the water, the faster the retrieve.

Many kinds of animal hair and feathers are used to tie these flies. Some tyers claim certain hair is better than others but I believe color is much more important than the kind of hair. I have caught trout on all kinds of streamer flies tied with both feathers and hair but if I were put in the position of having to fish with just one streamer I would have to pick one tied from marabou because of its action. When the fluffy marabou feathers become wet they have a tantalizing action that is difficult for trout to resist.

When fishing the bucktail or streamer, the size of the leader used is governed by the hook size and the type of water being fished, also the size of fish you might be lucky enough to catch! It would be foolhardy to use a large #2 fly on a light 4X or 5X leader. The leader would not be strong enough to stand the force of the strike necessary to set the hook. On the other hand, when one is using the small midget streamers or bucktails tied on size #10, #12, #14, or even #16 hooks, tapered leaders to 2X, 3X, or 4X may be used.

These flies are most frequently fished by casting across or down and across, and are retrieved by a hand twist or by stripping in line. Usually additional action is given by bringing the rod up in small jerks, sometimes as much as a foot, varying the retrieve as you bring the fly toward you. Sometimes waving the rod from side to side during the retrieve will help. If you are not getting strikes you must experiment with retrieves at various speeds. If a fish follows your fly and he fails to hit, speed up the retrieve and you may tempt it to strike. Here again I use the word "versatility." Try every kind of retrieve and combination of retrieves and you may change your luck.

I never change the fly until I have exhausted all the ways I know to fish the fly I have on the end of the leader; however, sometimes a change of fly to one smaller or larger may induce some trout to strike.

I prefer to fish with a bucktail or streamer with no weight built in the body, but depending on the water condition one may be forced to add weight. When weight is built in the body of the fly it will not have as much action as weight added to the leader six inches to a foot above the fly. If you want to be convinced, take a weighted fly and cast it into the water (preferably moving) and retrieve it in a normal fashion. Now take a fly, the same pattern without weight, and pinch on a split shot or wrap-around lead at least six inches above the fly. Use the same retrieve as you used on the weighted fly and you will readily see the difference. I believe this added action will excite many more trout to strike.

In most cases when the water is fairly clear, no weight is necessary in water only a few feet deep. If there are undercut banks, boulders, logs, or brush, one may be forced to add enough weight to get the fly to the proper level. You might encounter quite heavy riffles in water this deep, and here again, a fly fished near the bottom is usually the most productive. In deep pools the same may be true.

In the spring when the water is high or muddy, the bucktail or streamer must be fished near the bottom. My preference is to retrieve the fly slowly, just fast enough to keep from snagging on the bottom.

When weight is necessary I use mini shooting heads all the time simply because they are easier to cast and rarely snag the bottom. Some anglers prefer to fish with a sinking or Sink-Tip line and on a large stream or river this may be the best bet. Whenever possible I prefer a floating line because it is easier to pick up and cast. With the mini shooting heads I can usually get to any depth I desire.

There are a few rules that I follow as far as the color of flies is concerned and these rules are dictated by the color of the water. In discolored or muddy water I prefer a dark fly, usually black. In clear water a flashy bucktail or streamer is often very effective but it is still hard for me to believe flies that closely resemble the natural minnows in the stream are not the best.

I must admit as I get older I do not have the strong convictions I had as a younger man and as a result I am able to enjoy, experiment, and keep myself occupied the year round with this grand sport of fly fishing. The worst thing that can happen to any fly fisherman is for him to be self-satisfied and think he knows it all. When I get to this stage I will hang up my rod for good!

Mini Shooting Heads

Today the fly fisherman who fishes streamers, nymphs, or wet flies under the surface or on the bottom uses split shot in most cases. Sink-Tip and sinking lines help but personally I never cared much for them. For years, lead-core shooting heads have been used to fish the bottom for certain types of salt and freshwater fishing and where long casts were necessary, but for average stream fishing were not adequate.

The most annoying part of fishing when using split shot is frequent hang-ups or snags when fishing gravelly and rocky-bottom streams. Everyone who has ever used split shot knows what I am writing about. I have lost more streamers, nymphs, and wet flies as a result of snags than for any other reason. Now I feel this problem can be eliminated most of the time by the use of what I call mini lead-core shooting heads.

For the first six weeks of the 1983 trout season in Pennsylvania, all streams were running bank-full and fishing on or near the surface was futile. On the water I fished, almost everyone was forced to use so many split shot to get the streamers or nymphs down that they were often snagged on the bottom, taking away the pleasure of fly angling.

On the third day of the season I fished with Dr. Ralph Dougherty, a noted all-around fly fisherman. We had separated and when we met again I noticed a short piece of brown line incorporated in the lower part of his leader. When I asked him what it was, he told me he was experimenting with a piece of lead-core line to see if it would help eliminate the inconvenience caused when using split shot. He gave me a short piece about two feet long and asked me to try it and see what I thought about its use. I pulled out about two inches of the lead core on both ends, tied one end to the 1X section of my leader, tied a twelve-inch piece of 3X to the other end and then tied on a streamer fly.

After a few preliminary casts I was amazed at how easily I could cast with this combination. Since I was using a floating line, the pick-up was much smoother than with a sinking line I had tried the day before. While I fished the streamer with the lead core I did not hang up one time and I caught trout while others fishing the same stretch were continually catching the bottom.

On the way home I began to think of the possibilities of mini shooting heads. When I arrived home I called my friend Leon Chandler, then vice president of Cortland Line Company, and told him about my experience with the lead-core line. He was interested in the potential of the various sizes of small shooting heads and sent me a spool of vinyl-coated lead-core line. It was thirteen grains per foot and is sold in all pro shops under the name of L. C. 13.

When I received this line I immediately made up a series of small shooting heads from six inches to eight feet and the next day was out on the stream testing them under various conditions.

In heavy, riffly water that was up to four feet in depth, I used an eight-foot long shooting head tied to the 1X section of my leader, and to the end added about a foot of 3X. I fished both a streamer and nymph with phenomenal success. The streamer I fished down and across and never once had a hang-up. I could cast up to seventy feet with no effort. This combination was far superior for me to a Sink-Tip or sinking line.

For nymph fishing upstream in pocket water I used various lengths, depending on the speed of flow and depth of water. Here again, bottom snagging was practically nonexistent.

In some very fast pocket water I found that a nymph weighted with a few turns of lead wire worked a little better than one that was not weighted. The weighted nymph trailed better behind the lead core and made it easier to detect a strike.

When fishing a tandem of wet flies, I used the same length of terminal leader and attached the dropper and fly about ten inches back of the lead core. When it is necessary to keep the wet flies under the surface or deep during high-water periods, the depth and type of water determines the length of lead core to use, as in relatively shallow water one six inches long may be all that is needed. However, I have used the following sizes: six inches, twelve inches, eighteen inches, twenty-four inches, thirty-six inches, four feet, six feet, and eight feet. I have not used a dropper wet fly in back of sections longer than two feet.

So far I have only used this setup for trout. I am sure they would be great for the fly-rod man who fishes for shad. One could fish small streamers at any desired depth by using the correct length of lead-core line. The beauty of this technique is that one could cast about as far with the fly rod as most spin fishermen could cast using small shad darts.

When President Jimmy Carter was fishing Spruce Creek several years ago, the water was exceptionally high and one had to fish wet flies and nymphs most of the time to take trout. He used a small mini head with two wet flies and regularly caught trout. President Carter was impressed with this new concept and told me he was sure it would work well for getting the flies down for bluegills in Georgia.

The procedure for making the mini shooting heads from vinyl-covered lead-core line is as follows:

1. Cut lengths of lead core to suit your needs.
2. Attach desired length of nylon by using a nail knot. The leader on the end where you attach the fly should not be more than fifteen inches long.
3. Loop knots may be tied in nylon at each end of lead-core lines, then leader looped on. Lefty Kreh uses this method and thinks it saves time and is easy for those who have difficulty tying the blood knot.

Illustrations show this procedure:

LINE   LEADER   **MINI SHOOTING HEAD**   LEADER MATERIAL

NAIL KNOT   LEADCORE LINE   NOT MORE THAN 15''

VARIABLE LENGTH

ENDS MAY HAVE LOOP- LEFTY KREH'S METHOD

LEAD CORE LINE   LEADER MATERIAL

PULL TO TIGHTEN

REMOVE LEAD CORE — TELESCOPE LEADER MATERIAL INTO LEAD
CORE LINE. PENETRATE WALL WITH LEADER AND TIE NAIL KNOT

CUT-OFF

FINISHED KNOT

Length of the Mini Shooting Head depends on water depth and how close to the bottom you want to fish the fly.

5
Night Fishing

~~~~~~~~~~

FOR a certain breed of angler night fishing has a fascination that is difficult to describe in writing. It takes a man who enjoys solitude, who has patience, who is not afraid of snakes (in copperhead and rattlesnake country), who has no fear of the darkness, and who loves to catch big trout!

I believe the trout angler goes through several stages during his lifetime. First, the neophyte seems bound to kill his limit. He will spend long and tedious hours, in all kinds of weather, to attain this goal. Here the size of fish does not seem to matter much as long as they are of legal size. The next stage is where one concentrates on catching large trout and it is during this period the night fisherman is spawned. Some trout men never get beyond this second stage and will remain night fishermen until they can no longer get around after dark or until they make that last cast. The final stage, in my estimation, is the most enjoyable. It breeds new techniques, working toward perfection and knowledge. During this stage the angler becomes more concerned about conservation and the release of fine fish will be much more satisfying than filling the creel. He will enjoy angling in small mountain brooks where one seldom encounters much competition, as well as fishing the difficult stretches on our heavily fished limestone and freestone streams. At present, I am in the final stage but I still enjoy the second once in a while.

My night fishing experience began during the late nineteen-twenties. Most of the night fishing was done after the fifteenth of June. Incidentally, most of the large trout were concentrated in streams considered marginal. As the water warmed up in the lower reaches, the trout moved upstream until they found cooler water. Although I fished many small streams, most of the large trout were taken from Pennsylvania streams such as Pine Creek in Potter, Tioga, and Lycoming counties, and the Allegheny River, Mill Creek, and the Oswayo in Potter County. Hundreds were taken from the Goodsell Pool located in the town of Coudersport. All night fishermen should read Jim Bashline's book about this famous pool. The other streams were the Kinzua, north of Kane, Spring Creek, and Logan Branch in Centre County.

Trout can be taken at night on all types of flies but the wet fly has produced the most large trout for me. Although I have caught trout tied on hook sizes #6, #8, and #10, most of the flies I use are large. I prefer sizes from #4 to #2/0. My philosophy is, if you are after large trout, use the large flies! Of all the flies I have used, one stands out head and shoulders above the rest. Following is how I came to originate this pattern.

The trout that was slashing and racing all over the riffly water at the head of the long pool I was fishing had refused all the standard wet flies I had previously used for night fishing. My only deduction was that I needed a large fly and didn't have any. After a frustrating hour of casting, I decided to go home. As soon as I shucked my fishing clothes I headed for the fly-tying room and decided to tie a fly big enough to interest the trout I had heard that evening.

I clamped a large #2/0 Allcock hook in the vise and concocted a fly with a short tail, heavy palmered dubbed body, plus wings from the breast feathers of a Canada goose that were tied, one on each side, in front of the hackle so that the concave side faced the eye of the hook. The wingspan was over two inches. What a creature! I wondered if I would be able to cast it. I would soon find out.

The next evening after dinner I strung up a heavier rod with a matching line and a short seven-foot leader tapered to ten pounds. To this I tied on the fly. If I connected with that trout I was really going to stick it to him!

Since I had only about a four-mile drive to the stream I did not leave home until the sun started to settle on the horizon. All I could think of was the thrashing and splashing antics of that lunker brown. It seemed a long wait in the car until it was really dark, then I checked all my equipment, locked the car, and headed across the meadow to the head of the pool.

I sat down on the bank, made a few casts to see how the fly would react and must admit there was quite a fluttering noise as it whizzed past my ear, but I was satisfied because I could cast it across the stream to the far bank. I reeled in, laid the rod down at my side, and waited for some indication of the lunker starting to feed. I sat there for nearly an hour before I heard a gurgling noise near the far bank. At first I thought it was a muskrat submerging to enter its home but within a few seconds the water erupted in the center of the stream. This was what I was waiting for! Needless to say it didn't take me long to get in position above the trout. I stripped off twenty-five or thirty feet of line and as soon as I located the fish again, I cast above and beyond where I had heard the last splash.

As the fly swung downstream I retrieved with a very slow hand-twist and slight tip action. Before I fished out the cast the brown slashed after something almost under my rod tip. The fish was so close I was afraid of spooking it so I just held the fly motionless in the shallow, riffly water. Without any warning the rod was almost jerked out of my hand and the riffles exploded. The reel screamed as the trout raced to the tail end of the pool where it sulked. As fast as I could take in line, I moved down the bank until I was below the brown and began to apply pressure. The lunker dogged it for a few minutes then headed for the undercut bank on the far side of the pool. With the heavy leader I was using I pressured the fish back to the shallow tail end of the pool and played him there until he began to flounder in the shallows. I turned on my pencil flashlight, held it in my mouth, and pointed the beam on the trout. I said to myself "What a monster!" Now came the big decision: should I try to beach it or net it? The net looked mighty small but I decided it would be best under existing conditions. Applying all the pressure the rod would take, I eased him over the net and when I scooped he folded in the mesh. When I was thirty feet back from the stream I dumped out the net and gazed at the largest trout I had caught up to that time, a hook-jawed male brown, twenty-six inches long. Since that lunker I have caught hundreds more on the same fly pattern. The largest was a twenty-eight-and-one-half-incher that weighed eight and one-half pounds.

The pattern was so deadly on large brown trout that I kept it a secret for over fifteen years and then only showed it to a few close friends. It will outfish the conventional flies by so large a margin that all who have used this pattern will use no other when night fishing. In fact, the largest brown ever taken in Pennsylvania, a thirty-four-inch fifteen-pound five-ounce monster was taken on this pattern by my fishing companion, Joe Humphreys, who now teaches the angling courses I started at Pennsylvania State University in 1934.

Now for the first time I am going to tell all: How to tie and fish the fly that will outfish all other wet-fly patterns I have ever used for night fishing.

I believe the effectiveness of this fly is primarily related to the wings. They are tied in such a manner that they "push" water. In the slow-moving stretches and pools that hold most of the sizable browns, this fly will attract trout when most conventional patterns will be ignored. When large browns are cruising at night they sometimes cover a considerable area. In some of the long placid pools they move over a hundred yards or farther, up or down, from the undercut bank, brush pile, or daylight holding areas. As a result one must be patient when covering such water. I have taken most of the larger fish in two places: the shallow or riffly water at the head of the pool or at the shallow tail end. However, one cannot afford to skip the water between these two areas because you never know where you might hang one of these night feeders.

Generally I start fishing in the riffles at the head of a pool and may stay put in one spot for fifteen or twenty minutes before moving downstream a step or two. In the middle area of the pool I generally move faster, then spend about the same amount of time on the tail end of the pool as I did on the head end. If I know the pool holds a trophy trout I may repeat the above procedure for several hours.

One night, after fishing through a meadow on Spring Creek, I started for the car. I thought I would look over the water with my flashlight. In the riffles at the head of the first pool I spotted a large brown. I snapped off the light, moved above the trout, and presented the large wet fly. I held the fly stationary over the fish and he immediately smacked it! I have located more large trout with a flashlight than any other way. Many times when you put the light on a trout it will immediately leave. It is well to remember the next night you will no doubt find the trout in nearly the same place. Of course, the spotting of trout is not possible in large rivers and here one must pick the areas he thinks are the best.

When one locates one of the lunker browns, it can usually be taken if one has patience and fishes the water correctly. I should mention, and this is very important, the dark of the moon has produced most all of the large trout for me. In fact, I will not spend much time fishing when the moon is out at night and shining on the water. Sometimes it is possible to take fish before the moon comes up, or in a heavily shaded area, but as a general rule the fishing is usually poor; only on rare occasions have I had any exceptional luck during this time.

The night fisherman should be thoroughly acquainted with the area he is going to fish. If the stream is small enough to cast across one should know the length of line necessary to reach the far bank. One should know where the trees, bushes, and other obstacles are located. Otherwise, one would be hung up most of the time and soon lose interest and probably would spook any trout that was feeding.

When fishing this large night fly, cast across and slightly downstream. If the water is quite sluggish, I retrieve with a hand-twist and tip action. The retrieve must be slow! In riffly water, where the current gives action to the fly, the retrieve should be very slow; sometimes just holding the fly stationary is very effective. On the shallow flats at the tail end of the pools, retrieve just fast enough to keep the fly from snagging on the bottom. If one follows these suggestions, it will be almost impossible not to catch some fish.

At night you can use a leader heavy enough to handle most large trout. I generally use a tapered leader to ten-pound test. I have experimented with all sizes of leaders and never found any significant difference between the lighter and heavier leaders. The heavier leaders allow the angler to set the larger-size hook in the tough jaws of a lunker fish and to control the fish after it is hooked.

One thing I know for sure, once you hang a trophy brown at night you will be hooked too!

My philosophy concerning trout angling has changed dramatically over the years. As I grow older I am more concerned that future generations of anglers enjoy and experience quality fly fishing.

With the increasing number of people who are taking up the sport of angling, we need stringent regulations to reduce the kill. Limits must be reduced and more streams assigned for sport fishing where one must use artificial flies with barbless hooks. In other words, we need to educate our angling public that we must fish more for pleasure and recreation than for food.

In these chapters, as you have probably surmised, I have covered what I feel are the most important techniques in fishing dry, wet, nymph, night fly, and terrestrial. I have tried to keep all explanations and descriptions simple enough for everyone to understand. Also, I have tried to stress the point that fly fishing is not as complex as many writers have indicated. It is a sport all can learn and enjoy. In my fifty years of teaching I have never had one student who could not learn to cast, tie flies, and catch trout!

This book was written to try to help you in your learning experience. Remember, knowledge stored in your mind is yours forever. Sadly, what many anglers read is lost and usually never retained. I hope this won't happen to you.

Two

Techniques
of
Fly Tying

6

Tying Flies

~~~~~~~~

WHEN I first started tying flies sixty-eight years ago, fly tyers were as scarce as three-pound brook trout are today. The few professionals who knew anything about the art were so secretive that it was almost impossible to learn anything except what one could figure out for one's self.

Personally, I can think of no better hobby for the budding or accomplished trout fisherman than fly tying. The creative, artistic, and personal enjoyment derived from this hobby are sufficient in themselves, but these are only a part of it. This skill keeps us closely associated with angling during the off season and supplies a worthwhile and profitable recreation for our leisure time. Surely the trout fisherman who is proficient at both angling and fly tying will be much better prepared to meet the challenge of our heavily fished streams today.

Fly tying, contrary to the belief of many, is quite simple to master. Some tyers become more proficient than others, but I have never had one student who could not tie flies well enough to take trout.

I take pride in being able to state that I believe I have taught more people to tie flies than any other living individual. I have been teaching fly tying continuously since 1934 and in this span I have given instructions to well over eight thousand students. This experience, plus what I have learned from others, has convinced me that "haste makes waste" insofar as teaching fly tying is concerned. This section is written with this adage in mind, and I hope that beginners will find these simple techniques easy to follow and master. By the time we have finished they should be taking trout on their own creations.

There are many little tricks in fly tying every tyer picks up that to him seem best. However, many are quite difficult to describe. I will include only those that can be seen diagrammatically or can be described well enough for the majority to understand easily.

I want to make it clear that the diagrams are not supposed to be drawn to scale. This has been the trouble with all illustrations on fly tying I have ever seen. I want each diagram to show clearly each step so that even the beginner will have no difficulty following the procedure. Diagrams and descriptions will show the right-handed tyer.

Fly-Tying Materials

The tools and materials for the fly tyer are many. It is surprising how much can be accumulated in a very short time and how quickly all can be lost unless the proper precautions are taken against moths and beetles.

There are many catalogs available from reputable companies that supply materials and tools for the fly tyer. If you are interested in collecting, preserving, and dyeing your own material I suggest you purchase *Fly Tying Materials,* by Eric Leiser.

Tools: Vise, bobbin, scissors (preferably sharp-pointed), hackle pliers, and dubbing needle. In addition, if the pocketbook permits, one could purchase a whip-finisher, hackle gauge, scalpel, half-hitching tool, tweezers, flat-nosed pliers, and many other articles, but these are not really necessary.

Hooks: Sizes #8, #10, #12, #14, #16, #18, #20, and #22 with regular-length shanks and turned-down eyes (TDE), are the most popular hooks for dry and wet trout flies and nymphs. Sizes #2, #4, #6, #8, and #10 long-shank hooks for bucktail and streamer flies. Sizes #2 to #3/0 for bass bugs and flies for larger freshwater fish. Most freshwater hooks have a bronze finish.

Flies for salt water are usually tied on cadium-plated, nickel-plated, tinned, or stainless steel hooks to prevent the corrosive action of salt water. Here again, hook sizes from #4 to #3/0 are most popular. If you tie flies on hooks larger than #3/0 they are very difficult to cast.

Eventually you will need other hooks that are designed for specific flies, such as midges, spiders and Variants, nymphs, and so on.

Tying Thread: Nylon is the most popular thread used today. The be-

...nner should have several sizes from #2/0 to D for bucktails and ...reamers and #4/0 to #8/0 for smaller flies.

On all flies size #18 and smaller I use a fine monofilament that mikes ...ut at .002. This fine mono has a little stretch and this helps to bind in ...aterials very tight and does not build up bulk. The size of thread depends on the size of the fly being tied and the materials used. When tying flies on sizes #16 to #28, use the finest thread you can handle so as not to create a bulky fly or an excessively large head; however, when dressing large streamers, bucktails, deer-hair flies and bugs, or jigs you must use thread heavy enough to stand the pressure needed to secure the material. I use the smallest size thread possible for the fly I am tying because I can make many more turns without building up bulk. I believe this makes for a neater and stronger fly.

Hackle: The feathers used to tie dry and wet flies come most frequently from the neck of a chicken: the dry-fly hackle from the cock and the wet-fly hackle from the hen bird. The hackle when wound around the hook in front of the body makes the fibers stand out perpendicular to the shank of the hook. Of course there are other materials that are called hackle, such as any feather from any bird that has fibers the correct length for the hook you are tying on. Hair and even fine strands of rubber are called hackle; however, almost one hundred percent of all dry and wet flies are tied from chicken hackle.

In the past most fly tyers did not have the vaguest idea how to select a quality neck for tying flies. There are many colors and shades of hackle, and all can be used, but over ninety percent of all flies are tied from the following colors: dark ginger or brown, ginger, light ginger, grizzly, black, and blue dun. Of course, many dyed and some bleached hackle are used when natural colors are so scarce that the demand for them cannot be met. I do not like to use dyed or bleached hackle because of the effect on the feather. When a hackle is dyed or bleached the hackle becomes brittle, loses its natural oil, and will not take the punishment or last as long as a fly tied with the natural hackle. Only as a last resort will I use such a hackle.

The hen hackle used for wet flies has soft fibers that have a maximum amount of webbing. This soft hackle gives a breathing action to the fly that makes a wet fly very attractive to the fish. Even poor quality dry-fly hackle is not a good substitute for good hen hackle.

Since hackle is the most important material used in fly tying, you should be aware of the following when purchasing a cape. Stiff, vibrant, web-free hackle is required to tie high-floating dry flies and gives the angler numerous advantages. The more time your dry fly spends on the water, the greater your chances for success. Quality hackled flies can be dried with a minimum of false casts and quickly put back on the water, where it counts! Web-free hackle does not soak up water and its stiff supportive fibers assure that your fly will float consistently, cast after cast. These flies can withstand continued abuse from both the fish and prolonged casting and still retain their original form. You will fish with confidence knowing that your fly will float high and dry.

Fly tying is much more enjoyable when one is using quality hackle and the end product is a better looking and floating dry fly; on the other hand, inferior hackle can be very difficult to work with. Problems such as short hackle length, breakage, and twisting can turn a relaxed session of fly tying into a frustrating experience. Quality hackle will have quills that are flexible enough to be wound without twisting. They will be long and narrow with short, stiff, glossy fibers. This allows the tyer to use just two, and on rare occasions one, hackles for a well-dressed fly, providing the obvious economic benefit of more flies per neck. If you are a novice, quality hackle helps you to progress faster toward tying better flies. If you are an experienced tyer, the hackle you use reflects your work-manship.

There are three steps in examining a neck to check for hackle quality.

1. Lay the neck in your hand with the narrow portion (nape) of the neck toward you and observe the overall appearance (see photo 1). The hackles down the center line of the neck should lay relatively straight. The side or throat hackles will usually have a slight curve to them. The neck should be uniformly and thickly hackled with the hackles being narrow and vibrant in appearance. The skin should be flexible to aid in hackle selection and easy removal during tying. The overall appearance should be pleasing and consistent.

2. Flex the neck at the point where it begins to widen, (see photo 2). This area will contain the hackles that are most commonly used for trout flies. This flexing of the neck allows you to check the specific size group of hackle for quality. There should be a minimum of broken tips and stems. Only a few, if any, pin (incompletely devel-

oped) feathers should be present. Check to be sure the neck has a generous number of hackles in the desired tying range (see photo 3).

3. Select an individual feather for further examination (see photo 4). You need not pluck the feather off the neck, simply separate it from its companions. Check the web line to be sure there is not excessive webbiness in the useful portion of the hackle. Bend the hackle in an arc (see photo 5). The fibers should be short in relation to the length of the stem. The individual fibers should be stiff and uniform. Stiff, web-free fibers will stand independently from the center stem and will spring back into position when flicked with your finger. The fibers should be dense and of uniform length along the useful portion of the stem. Last, check the center stem for flexibility. A flexible stem will be a definite advantage in winding (see photo 6).

When you select a neck you must determine the neck's intended use. The fly patterns and hackle-size range you wish to tie will determine the colors and shades required and help you select the necks that will be your best value.

The finest quality hackle in the world is raised in Belleville, Pennsylvania, by the Metz Hatchery. I am glad I played a small part in getting this quality production started. It started when Dave Engerbretson introduced me to Andy Minor of St. Paul, Minnesota. Andy graciously gave me twelve dozen eggs that I turned over to Bucky Metz. He was going to raise enough birds for hackle that he and I would use, but then decided to go commercial. He has improved the quality tenfold by selective breeding and is continually breeding for better quality. Bucky alone is responsible for the operation and its development. Metz hackle is now being sold at leading retailers and suppliers throughout the world. What follows is the grading methods used at the Metz hatchery.

Grade Number 1 necks will have a full range of hackle from size #8 through #24 (and often as small as #28). They will be full and thick with long and narrow, virtually web-free, hackle. The hackle will be glossly, springy, and stiff. Fiber density will be very pronounced. Coloration will be pleasing and consistent. These are by far the best capes available in the world and a pride to own.

Grade Number 2 necks are almost identical in quality to Number 1

1

2

3

4

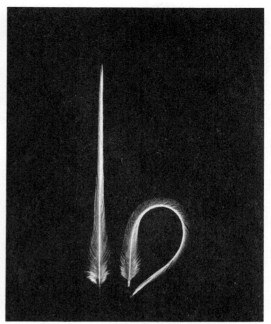

5   6

but may not be quite as heavily hackled and perhaps slightly webbier. You may also find an occasional pin feather or broken tip. However, since grading standards are so stringent, none of these flaws will be significant. Selling at a considerable price reduction from Number 1, but essentially the same quality hackle, they are a great value.

Grade Number 3 necks may have a little more web, broken tips, or pin feathers than Number 2, but still have top-quality dry-fly hackle. They may not be as heavily hackled in the smaller hook sizes (#18 and smaller), but may be very full with premium quality hackle in the more commonly used sizes (#16 and larger). These necks make a fine choice for the novice or commercial fly tyer.

Body Materials: In recent years so many new synthetic materials are being used for bodies and wings that I recommend you send for catalogs from several supply houses. This way you can keep abreast of what is being used. However, the old reliable materials that have been used by most master tyers still head the list for me: silk floss, yarns, chenille, peacock herl and eye quill, tinsel, mylar tubing, and fur from any animal that is fine enough to be spun on for dubbing. Fur can be bleached, dyed, and blended to create any desired color. Stripped hackle quill makes one of the most durable bodies. Deer, elk, moose, antelope, and goat hair is used for bodies and wings. In fact, any material that can be wound or tied on a hook can be used. Experiment!

Wing Material: Wing quills (from any bird) may be used depending on color. Duck quills are most frequently used, breast and side feathers from mallard, wood duck, and teal, as well as deer hair, squirrel, badger, groundhog, and many others. Wing quills used for dry-fly wings have never really been satisfactory because with very little use the fibers separate. The wood-duck and other flank feathers, hairwings, and hackle tips used on many patterns are much better and until recently were the only ones used for what we call the divided and spent wings on dry flies.

Six or eight years ago I was over at the Metz Hatchery watching the caping of hackle birds. Some hen saddles were on the drying boards. In addition there were some neck trimmings available and I acquired some of both for experimental purposes. As soon as I arrived home I tied up some dry flies using the fibers stripped from the hen saddles (same procedure as wood duck) for wings on conventional patterns. The results were phenomenal! The first flies I tried were dry light Cahills. The light-speckled hen saddle feathers made beautiful wings and I could see the fly much better than the standard pattern.

I have used hen saddle patches and neck trimmings for dry and wet flies in the following colors: white, brown, light and dark speckled ginger, various shades of brown speckled, light ginger, all shades of blue dun, black grizzly, and white dyed fluorescent orange, hot pink, yellow, and green. More about these wings later.

I have never been one to put in print anything until I was satisfied in my own mind of its worth. I am now convinced that this winging material is equal to or better than any on the market today. Not only do they look great but once they are dressed with a floatant will float indefinitely.

Body and hen saddle feathers have been used for cut and burnt wings for many years; however, for upright wings, they have never been satisfactory for me. They will cause the fly to spin and twist the leader on flies as small as #22. On down-wing dry flies (ants, caddis, grasshoppers, and nymph wing pads) they are excellent because no twisting occurs. Every fly fisherman and fly tyer who has seen and used the flies tied with this material is as enthusiastic about it as I am.

Tails: Throat and spade hackles are best for dry flies. Use materials listed for other type flies. Metz now supplies small packs of spade hackle in all colors that are excellent for Matuka streamers and tails on all types of wets, dry flies, and nymphs.

Bucktail and Streamer Flies: Saddle and large dry-fly hackles are most frequently used for feather-wing streamers. For Matuka streamers, I prefer hen saddle feathers. Deer hair is most commonly used for bucktails but hair from any animal that is long enough and the desired color may be used. Marabou, the fluffy underfeather from the turkey, is dyed all colors and is one of the best materials used on the streamer flies because of the undulating action when fished.

Head Cement: Finish off a fly with some waterproof lacquer or a good head cement. A fast-drying cement is most popular. I use a mixture of approximately one-third Shoe Goo and two-thirds toluene. This will give you a consistency about the same as a thin lacquer. You may need to delete or add a little more to get it to your liking. I like it thick enough so that when I insert the point of a dubbing needle in the solution a tiny drop will adhere to the point. This is important when working with small flies and a small amount of sealant is needed. This mixture is so superior to lacquer that once you use it you will rarely, if ever, use lacquer again.

If you want to make a test, take a knife blade or dubbing needle, insert it in a bottle of lacquer, drain and let dry. Do the same with the Shoe Goo solution. You will be able to scrape off the lacquer by stroking a few times with the non-cutting edge of your fly-tying scissors. Try this same experiment with the Shoe Goo solution. It is practically impossible to remove it without dipping in the solvent. I have experimented with this sealant since 1981 and know what I write is no hearsay. Most fly-tying material companies list a flexible sealant under a number of trade names. They are all good.

Many fly tyers do not realize that waxed thread was first used by Scotch and English tyers. The thread was waxed enough to hold it in place between operations. This was necessary because the early tyers held the hook between the thumb and index finger, so no weight was used to hold the thread taut. Early American tyers used this technique and waxed thread is still used by most present-day tyers. Since the invention of the fly-tying vise and bobbin I have never cared for prewaxed thread and have not used it for at least forty years. It can be a nuisance when it clogs the neck of the bobbin and if too heavy will sometimes change the color of some body materials, especially silk. Since experimenting with the Shoe Goo solution I use it on many operations and know it makes for a more secure fly.

Now, how does this pertain to the fly tyer?

First: After winding on the tying thread I apply a light coat of the sealant, this keeps the thread from turning on the hook.

Second: It dries faster than lacquer and is a much better sealant for finishing off the head of the fly. Be sure not to get any in the eye of the hook. If you do, immediately clear it by running the dubbing needle through the eye.

Third: Peacock eye quill has never been very substantial. Sometimes it will break or split when you catch the first fish. If you give the peacock quill a light coat of this solution it will not change the color and will prolong the life of the fly many times. I have caught over three dozen trout on one quill fly and it was still in good condition.

Fourth: Now when I am using dubbing for body material, especially on small flies, I immerse my dubbing needle in the solution, rub it lightly up and down on the tying thread, and immediately spin on the dubbing. When you first try this method you will be surprised because the dubbing will not slide or move on the thread. In addition, when spinning on the dubbing, by pressure between the thumb and finger you can make the dubbing as fuzzy or tight as you wish.

Fifth: When tying bucktails, after making the first two or three turns I usually cut off the excess at the head of the fly. Some tyers put a drop of lacquer on at this time or else work the tying thread back through the protruding cut ends of the bucktail. This was the best method but still many bucktails would gradually come apart. Now, when you reach this stage, take a drop of the Shoe Goo solution and work it with the dubbing needle in the stump end of the bucktail. Work the threads through the protruding ends and continue to finish off the head. Let dry. Now you have a bucktail, if you follow the procedure, that is practically impossible to pull apart.

Sixth: On any down-wing (wings on grasshoppers, wet flies, burnt wings for dry caddis), a very light coating of this cement will keep the wings from fraying and in shape for an indefinite length of time and will prolong the life of deer-hair ants and deer-hair inchworms. I use a small brush made from hackle fibers for this operation. I might add I have experimented by using a very light coating on dry-fly quill wings to keep the wings from splitting, but because of the stiffness this sometimes has a tendency to spin the fly, especially when I am using a fine terminal tippet.

Seventh: In addition, when I tie in hackle by the stump end I always put a tiny drop of solution after the first wind. More about this later.

There will undoubtedly be more uses found for this cement as others begin to experiment but these are the most important I have found up to the present time.

This list is by no means complete but will be sufficient for any beginner. Remember, if you are a beginner, it is not necessary to have all the materials listed. Use what you have and add to your supply as you are able. A sample fly as a model would be a great help for the beginner.

Diagram 1 shows the important parts of a hook and how to select hackle in relation to the size of the hook. For any regular fly, both wet and dry, this rule holds true. The hackle fibers should be from one and one-half to two times as long as the gap of the hook you are tying on. It is best to gauge the hackle by selecting fibers in the center third or middle of the hackle. The *bend* is the point where the hook starts its downward turn. The *eye* is at the front end and the bend at the rear of the hook.

Diagram 2 shows the various grades of hackle. Any feather from any bird, if the fibers are long or short enough for the size hook you are tying on, can be used for wet-fly hackle; however, ninety-nine percent of all dry flies are tied from cock's hackle. Here we want a hackle that is long (from tip to stump end) with short, glossy fibers that have a minimum of down or webbing and with a mid-rib that is flexible enough to be wound on without twisting. If you take a cock's hackle and hold it against a contrasting background, you can easily see the webbing on the fibers. This is illustrated by the small circle in the diagram. If the hackle has only a small dense area of webbing near the stump end as illustrated by **Diagram 1-A** and the rest of the fibers are clear, you have a super quality hackle. **Diagram 1-B** and **Diagram 1-C** are still very good quality hackle. **Diagram 1-D** should only be used for wet flies unless no other is available.

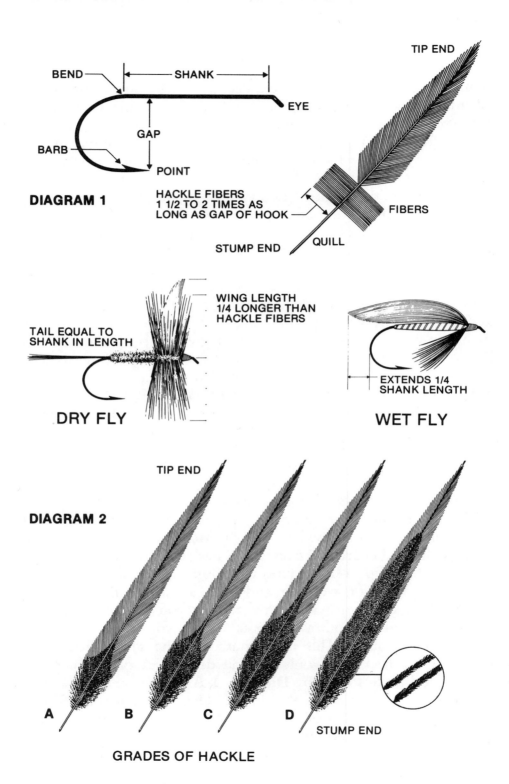

BEND

SHANK

EYE

GAP

BARB

POINT

DIAGRAM 1

TIP END

HACKLE FIBERS
1 1/2 TO 2 TIMES AS
LONG AS GAP OF HOOK

FIBERS

STUMP END

QUILL

WING LENGTH
1/4 LONGER THAN
HACKLE FIBERS

TAIL EQUAL TO
SHANK IN LENGTH

DRY FLY

EXTENDS 1/4
SHANK LENGTH

WET FLY

TIP END

DIAGRAM 2

A   **B**   **C**   **D**

STUMP END

GRADES OF HACKLE

The neophyte fly tyer's greatest temptation is the urge to advance too rapidly. It is quite easy for anyone to tie quality flies if time is taken with the fundamentals and if each step is mastered before going on to the next. Most anglers who are fly tyers take pride in their handiwork and take great pains to make each fly a work of art. They proudly display their creations to fellow anglers and wait for the praise they justly deserve.

7

Fluorescent Flies

~~~~~~~~~~

SINCE I retired in January 1973 I have had time to really experiment and put together new techniques in fishing and fly tying. Some of these experiments have changed lifelong beliefs that most anglers still accept as cold, hard facts.

In the past I believed that exact imitations of natural insects, aquatic or terrestrial, were of the utmost importance, especially in size and color. I still believe that to be true in most cases. Body and hackle color are essential in imitating natural insects. However, I am convinced that wing color does not make any difference to the trout.

Although there is a difference of opinion among some fly anglers of the value of wings, I do believe they make a difference. The hackleless flies prove this and I tie all my flies with wings because I feel silhouette is important. To me, a fly without wings just doesn't seem right. I might add that the fly tyers I know who eliminate wings are usually the ones who have difficulty tying a good winged fly.

Since I have an eye problem, it is difficult for me to see and follow some dry flies floating on the surface. The problem has been especially troublesome with the smaller flies, and in some light conditions I could not see the fly at all. All I could do was strike when I saw a rise where I thought my fly should be. It was difficult to know whether I was getting a drag-free float, the most important element in dry-fly fishing.

Forty years ago I tied a Green Drake pattern using fluorescent calf tail for wings and I was able to see the fly better than any pattern I had tied before. I still use the same pattern, as do many others who have seen it perform. Until the spring of 1983 I had never used any other fluorescent material for wings. Then, in May of that year, I was given some Metz hen saddle patches dyed fluorescent orange, hot pink, yellow, and green. Since I had been using colored hen saddle patches for divided wings on some dry-fly patterns I most frequently use, I decided to see if the fluorescent wings would help me to see the flies and find out how the trout would react to the brilliant colors.

The first fly I experimented with was a deer-hair ant. I wanted to see how the burnt wing compared with the fluorescent red lacquer I had been using on the back to make the fly more visible. The first wing I tied was hot pink. I could see the fly twice as far as I could the lacquered version, and the wing was still visible when the deer hair was practically torn apart. This discovery was worth the experiment because deer-hair ants are usually better fish-takers when they are broken up and fuzzy looking.

It was a phenomenal experience to see trout rise and take fluorescent flies without any hesitation. The best part was that I could see the flies in quiet or riffly water and missed very few rises. It turned the frustration I had been experiencing into delightful days astream again.

The Adams, Cahill, Hendrickson, Quill Gordon, Spruce Creek, and Sulphur flies have always been on my list of favorite patterns and all but the Cahills and Sulphurs were very difficult for me to see, so I tied the flies according to the original pattern but substituted the various colored wings. I alternated the original patterns with the fluorescent-winged flies and found the new flies worked equally well.

Trout are more selective during the *Tricorythodes* hatch, but here again, fluorescent-winged duns and spinners were not rejected.

I tied fluorescent divided wings on almost all the flies I used, not only in Pennsylvania but also for the most productive patterns I fish in the West Yellowstone area. Fishing a caddis on the Madison below Quake Lake, I could follow the fluorescent hot pink fly in riffly and pocket water, and as a result I could catch the majority of the rising trout.

On many small mountain streams overgrown with rhododendron, other trees, and shrubs, the light is so dim it is difficult to see a fly beneath the foliage. Joe Humphreys and I gave the fluorescent-wing deer ants a real test on such a stream and the results were even better than I had hoped for. When certain light conditions exist, especially in dense, shaded areas, we were able to see the green fluorescent wings a little better. On most bright, sunny days I can follow flies #16 and larger and use regular patterns; however, the smaller flies give me problems, and as a result I will never be without some fluorescent-winged flies.

I am not suggesting that the flourescent-wing flies are better than the traditional feathers used on original patterns, but for those of us who have trouble following the drifting flies they are a godsend.

One of the most popular wings for dry flies are hackle tips from rooster necks. Hackle from imported and domestic chickens was the primary source for these wings and most of the tips had nice rounded ends and made excellent wings. For the past sixteen years most of the prime hackle has been raised commercially in the United States and the quality is continually improving by selective breeding. As a result it is getting difficult to find capes that have satisfactory hackle tips for wings because the top-quality necks have long, narrow, sharp-pointed hackle. The cut and burnt wings never proved satisfactory for upright and spent wings because when cast they would usually spin and twist the leader.

For the past eight years or so I have resorted to using hen hackle tips for wings because of the more rounded ends, but they, too, are becoming sharp-pointed because of selective breeding.

Recently I picked up some hen saddle hackle to dye for fluorescent wings. When I returned home I discovered a distinct change in the conformity of the feathers. These feathers were quite different from the wide, rounded ones I had used for divided wings by stripping off the long fibers. These new saddle feathers were narrower at the terminal ends and the fibers were short. I felt sure I could use the feathers for upright and spentwing flies and there would be more body and the silhouette would be greatly improved.

I immediately tied up a dozen flies using the feathers. They looked great and the wide range of colors allowed me to tie many different patterns. If they could pass two tests they would be a great asset for fly tyers. So, I went out in my front yard with a ten-foot leader tapered to 5X, and tied on a #12 fly. I made many false casts and casts up to sixty feet and never once did the wings twist the leader. The soft and flexible quill was the answer. During the next few weeks I caught many trout on the flies and the wings held up as well as the hackle tips.

All hen saddles are showing this change, but some are more advanced.

However, enough are narrow-tipped to allow the fly tyer to tie almost all patterns used today. I hope enough hen saddles will be available to meet the demand. All fly fishermen who have seen the dry flies I have tied using these feather tips share my enthusiasm. I feel quite sure they will be more popular than the narrow rooster hackle.

8

Tying the Hackle Wet Fly

~~~~~~~~~

BEFORE tying any fly always bend down the barb if you are not using barbless hooks.

Diagram 3. The hook should be placed in the vise (represented by the dotted line) so the point of the hook is covered, allowing as much clearance between the top of the vise and shank of the hook as possible. The tyer should be seated directly in front of the vise. Now we are ready to begin.

There are many different types of fly-tying bobbins. I like one that is light in weight so that the finest of tying thread will hold it when suspended.

Note how this bobbin is held, with the thumb on the spool and held by the fingers. If another type of bobbin is used, hold it with the fingers. Never hold any bobbin back in the palm of the hand. I suggest the beginner start with 3-0 or 4-0 tying thread.

Take the end of the tying thread between the thumb and first finger of the left hand, holding the bobbin in the right hand and allowing about three inches of tying thread between the bobbin and the left hand. Lay tying thread over the top of the hook. Start winding clockwise on the shank, beginning one-fifth the distance back of the eye, making a few turns toward the eye. Hold tying thread firmly in the left hand and wind back over your initial turns; continue back to one-third the distance in front of the bend and cut off the protruding end of tying thread. Now, wind back to the bend, keeping each wind close together, then wind back to the middle of the shank. It would now be a good idea to turn to the explanation of **Diagram 10** and practice a few of the half-hitches. If you wait until you are ready to finish the fly to learn this step you may find yourself in trouble.

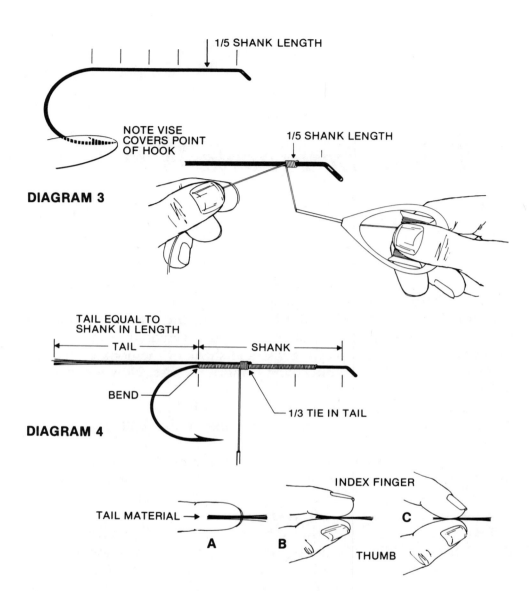

1/5 SHANK LENGTH

NOTE VISE
COVERS POINT
OF HOOK

1/5 SHANK LENGTH

DIAGRAM 3

TAIL EQUAL TO
SHANK IN LENGTH

|← TAIL →|← SHANK →|

BEND

1/3 TIE IN TAIL

DIAGRAM 4

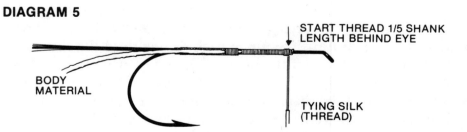

TAIL MATERIAL →

INDEX FINGER

A **B** **C**

THUMB

DIAGRAM 5

START THREAD 1/5 SHANK
LENGTH BEHIND EYE

BODY
MATERIAL

TYING SILK
(THREAD)

Diagram 4. From a large hackle, strip off four to six fibers for the tail. Be sure to keep the tip ends even. Remember, the tail should be as long as the shank of the hook on all regular length shanks, but this sometimes varies. The small diagrams show how to hold the tail. **Diagram 4-A** shows the position of the tail on the index finger. **Diagram 4-B** shows how to hold it so that the ends of thumb and finger are even.

The tying thread should be about one-third from the bend of the hook before you start to tie in the tail. Hold the tail on top of the hook so that the fibers are flat on the shank, with the ends of thumb and finger apart as in **Diagram 4-B.** Now bring the tying thread up between the thumb and tail material, but back far enough so that it can be held between the thumb and finger. Then bring the thread over the top of the tail and shank of the hook and down the other side between the tail and the index finger. Before you draw the tying thread up, close the thumb and finger as in **Diagram 4-C.** This should hold the tail secure on top of the shank of the hook. Make several more turns with the tying thread as diagrammed, winding the thread over the tail and back to the bend of the hook. Be sure to hold the tail directly on top of the shank.

Diagram 5. Select body material. Single or untwisted silk floss or chenille is best for the beginner. Tie in body material with a few turns of the tying thread just in front of the tail and continue winding the tying thread up to one-fourth the length of the shank, back of the eye. Remember, body material and all other materials should be held, when tying, in the same manner as the tail fibers were held.

Diagram 6. When winding body material to the right, use the right hand to take the material over the top of the shank and the left to pick it up and take it under. If it is necessary to wind back to the left, as may happen when building up the body, reverse the above using the left hand over the top and the right under.

For the wet fly, build a tapered body as shown by **Diagram 7** and run the body up to the tying thread.

Diagram 7. When this step is reached you should be holding the body material between the thumb and finger of the left hand. Now pass the tying thread under the body material and change hands, bobbin in the left hand, body material in the right. Wind tying thread over the top of the body material as shown by the dotted lines. Take several turns, up

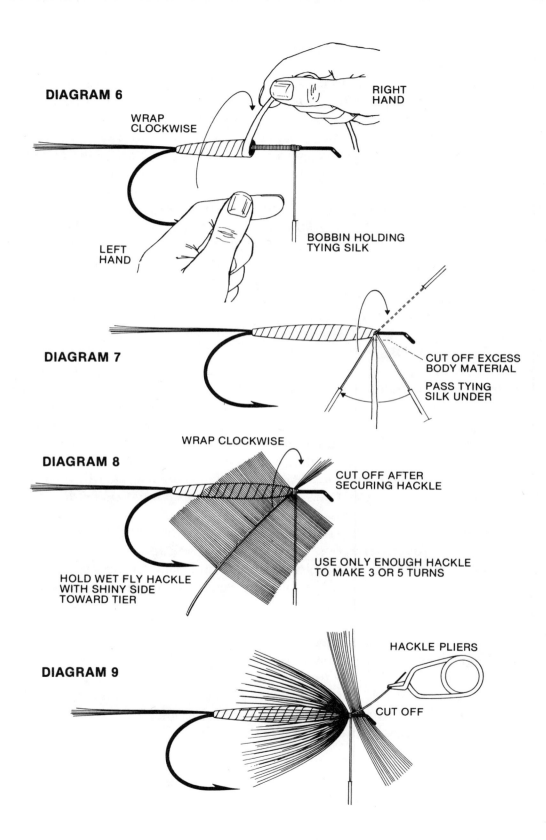

DIAGRAM 6

WRAP
CLOCKWISE

RIGHT
HAND

LEFT
HAND

BOBBIN HOLDING
TYING SILK

DIAGRAM 7

CUT OFF EXCESS
BODY MATERIAL

PASS TYING
SILK UNDER

WRAP CLOCKWISE

DIAGRAM 8

CUT OFF AFTER
SECURING HACKLE

USE ONLY ENOUGH HACKLE
TO MAKE 3 OR 5 TURNS

HOLD WET FLY HACKLE
WITH SHINY SIDE
TOWARD TIER

HACKLE PLIERS

DIAGRAM 9

CUT OFF

as close to the body as possible. Now cut off excess body material. Be sure not to cut your tying thread.

Diagram 8. Select wet-fly hackle that has fibers the right length for the size hook you are using. Remember, the fibers should be one and one-half to two times as long as the gap of the hook. Hold by the tip end and stroke the fibers between the thumb and index finger, working from the tip toward the stump end. The purpose of this stroking is to make the fibers stand out perpendicular to the quill. Strip off fibers from the stump end, leaving enough to make three to five winds around the shank. Tie the tip end of the hackle close to the body so that the top or shiny side of the hackle is on top facing out. Take enough turns around the tip end of the hackle so it will not pull out. Tying thread should now be almost up to the eye of the hook. Cut off any protruding hackle-tip end.

Grasp the stump end of the hackle with hackle pliers prior to winding the hackle around the shank of the hook. When winding the hackle, use hands in the same manner as when winding the body. As each turn of the hackle is made, its fibers should be stroked back. this can easily be accomplished by holding the hackle pliers in the right hand while using the thumb and the first two fingers of the left hand to stroke back the hackle. Make your first turn as close to the body as possible, keeping the top or shiny side of the hackle facing the eye of the hook. Make your second turn close in front and repeat. Three to five turns of the hackle are sufficient for any wet fly. Gauge hackle length so you can tie off on the quill.

Diagram 9. After three to five turns have been made, end with the hackle on top and in the right hand. Hold in this position and bring the tying thread up and over in the manner used to secure the body. Cut off the excess stump end and make enough additional turns with the tying thread to cover all visible material.

Diagram 10. We are now ready to finish the fly. This diagram shows the half-hitch knot. Remember, now as in all operations, the tying thread must be held firmly so it will not unwind.

I suggested earlier that you practice the half-hitch. I will describe the knot. Hold the bobbin in the left hand so about three inches of tying thread is between the left hand and the hook. Grasp the tying thread between the bobbin and hook, up close to the body, with the tips of the

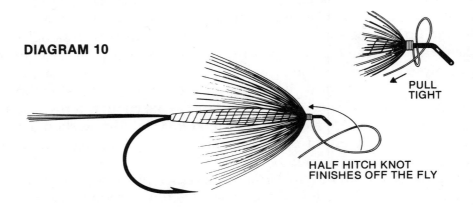

DIAGRAM 10

PULL
TIGHT

HALF HITCH KNOT
FINISHES OFF THE FLY

index finger and the thumb of the right hand. The nail of the index finger should be facing you. Holding the tying thread secure in your right hand and slackening the thread from your bobbin hand, make a half turn clockwise with your right hand, dropping the loop formed over the eye of the hook. Three half-hitches are usually sufficient. Be sure the loop is drawn up tight. A half-hitching tool can be purchased for a nominal fee and is easy to use. It is well worth the investment. Later on I will describe the whip-finish. Complete the fly with a drop of sealant on the head.

9

Fly Bodies

～～～～～

THERE are many materials used for fly bodies. Any material that can be wound on the shank of a hook may be used, but the most common are silk floss, fur and synthetic fiber dubbing, quill, chenille, synthetic fiber yarns, and wool. Of all body materials, I believe the poorest is wool. I never use it, substituting the synthetics or using dubbing, either natural or dyed. Quills from the eye of an eyed peacock feather are the quills most frequently used, but hackle quill and quill stripped from primary flight feathers (duck quills) and others are not uncommon.

To prepare peacock eye quills for use, one must remove the fluff from the quill. Lay the quill on a table with a light background. Hold by the tip and stroke toward the butt end with a soft eraser. For most flies, two inches of quill is sufficient. If you try to remove the fluff from the entire quill the upper half frequently breaks. The butt end is the strongest and widest and is the part to use. If the quills are soaked in water for a half hour the fluff can easily be stripped by sliding the fibers between the nails of the index finger and thumb or the edge of a scissor blade and thumb. The entire eye may be submerged in Clorox or other suitable bleaching solution. Be sure to remove the eye from the solution as soon as the fluff is dissolved and immerse it in a solution of baking soda and water. After the eye has dried it may be rubbed gently with light oil.

Hackle quill is by far the most substantial and I like to use it whenever possible. To prepare the quill, strip the fibers from a large neck or saddle hackle. Now, soak the quill for at least an hour in water. While still moist, tie in by its small end and wind on so that each turn is as tight as possible against the preceding one. Never overlap. This type of quill gives an even-tapered body. A thin coat of sealant over the body will help show up the segmentation more clearly.

It is well to remember when using any quill or tinsel for bodies that the shank of the hook should be as smooth as possible. Any irregularities that show up after tying in the tail should be filled in with tying thread. When chenille is used for bodies, it is best to shred the end and tie in by two exposed threads. This way you avoid irregularities or humps in the body.

The dubbed or fur body is very popular. By blending different colored fur almost any shade can be obtained. Fur from any animal, if it is soft enough, may be used.

To prepare fur for dubbing, first pull out all long guard hairs so that only the soft silky underfur remains. If the natural color is to be used, the underfur may be left on the hide until ready to be used. However, I prefer to cut enough of the soft underfur to dub a few hundred bodies, and I store it in a small plastic bag. Dyed or natural fur may be used if one wants to blend several colors. Mix them by pulling out or cutting off a little of each color, close to the hide. Lay them together and pull apart, lay them back together and repeat until the original colors are blended to a new shade. Blending may be simplified if you have access to an electric mixer. Take the colors to be blended, drop in the container, set to mix, turn on, and the dubbing will be blended in just a few seconds. With both methods you may have to add a little extra of one or more colors to get the desired shade.

All fly bodies are wrapped on in precisely the same manner. They may vary in thickness and taper of course, but the procedure is the same.

Diagram 11 illustrates the ribbed body. It shows the procedure and the correct order in which the body and ribbing material are tied on.

After the tail is secured, work the tying thread to the bend and tie in ribbing material here **(Diagram 11-A).** Now tie in the body material, **(Diagram 11-B)** and spiral the tying thread up to one-third the distance in back of the eye. Wind body material and tie off as previously described. Next, spiral ribbing over the body and tie off **(Diagram 11-C).** For the dry fly I prefer to have the body slightly tapered from the front to the rear end.

Some fly tyers have trouble with the ribbing. In fact, many believe it is impossible to wind the ribbing so it will not slip. To overcome this

DIAGRAM 11

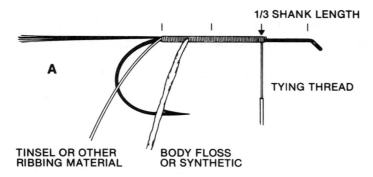

A

1/3 SHANK LENGTH

TYING THREAD

TINSEL OR OTHER
RIBBING MATERIAL

BODY FLOSS
OR SYNTHETIC

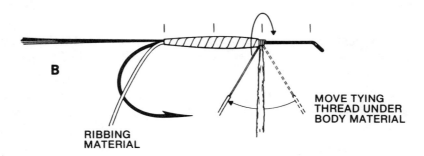

B

RIBBING
MATERIAL

MOVE TYING
THREAD UNDER
BODY MATERIAL

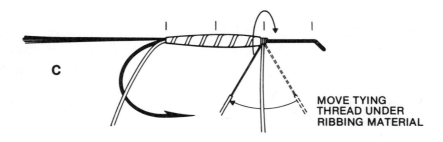

C

MOVE TYING
THREAD UNDER
RIBBING MATERIAL

difficulty, do not take any extra turns around the butt end of the body before spiraling is started, and do not make any turns in front of the body before tying off. Start to spiral the ribbing material immediately, and when the front end of the body is reached tie it off at once. In addition, the spirals should be the same distance apart on bodies that have the same diameter. On tapered bodies the spirals should be progressively wider as one winds from the rear to the front of the body. A little experimenting on the part of any tyer will soon iron out this technique.

Diagram 12. There are many methods commonly used for fixing dubbed bodies. Diagram 12 shows the easiest and one of the best methods. After the tail is secured, work the tying thread to the position shown, one-fourth the way up from the bend. Hold the tying thread taut with the left hand three or four inches below the shank of the hook. To attach the dubbing to the tying thread, take a little fur between the thumb and finger of the right hand and lay it on the underside of the tying thread, close to the shank of the hook. The index finger, at the first joint, should be placed under the dubbing to hold against the tying thread. Now squeeze tightly with the tip of the thumb as shown and spin smoothly until the tip of the thumb reaches beyond the end of the index finger. Reverse this operation without releasing pressure. Release thumb and finger to take a little more dubbing and spin on below the first. Repeat until you feel you have enough for the body. I like the dubbing to be spun on the tying thread in a spindle shape with a longer taper at each end, as shown in **Diagram 13.** After you have dubbed several dozen bodies, you will have no difficulty judging the correct amount of fur to use. Some feel wax is beneficial if applied before spinning on the dubbing, but I believe they are following an old tradition passed on by the English tyers who did not have the advantage of a bobbin. I have no use for wax of any kind for any fly-tying operation. I always use a small drop of Shoe Goo solution or flexible cement rubbed on the tying thread with the dubbing needle. This will keep the dubbing from slipping on the thread and is very useful at times.

Diagram 13. You now have the dubbing secured to the tying thread. Notice you have a little space between the top of the dubbing and the shank of the hook. Take the bobbin in your right hand and take up the excess tying thread until the dubbing just reaches the neck of the

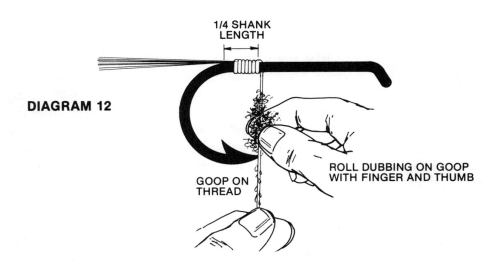

DIAGRAM 12

1/4 SHANK LENGTH

GOOP ON THREAD

ROLL DUBBING ON GOOP WITH FINGER AND THUMB

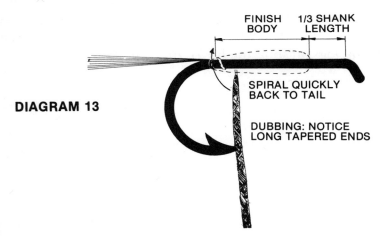

DIAGRAM 13

FINISH BODY

1/3 SHANK LENGTH

SPIRAL QUICKLY BACK TO TAIL

DUBBING: NOTICE LONG TAPERED ENDS

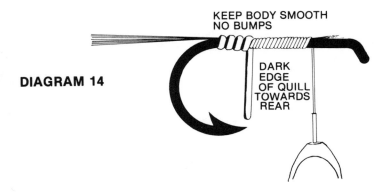

DIAGRAM 14

KEEP BODY SMOOTH NO BUMPS

DARK EDGE OF QUILL TOWARDS REAR

bobbin. Wind back the free tying thread to the bend of the hook and wind the body just prepared toward the eye, building up the body with a slight taper as shown by the dotted line, overlapping if necessary. Stop one-third the distance in back of the eye. If you have too much dubbing for the size hook you are tying on, pick off the excess with the thumb and forefinger of your right hand. If you want the body to be fuzzy, as is often the case, take a dubbing needle and pick out fur until you have the desired effect.

Diagram 14. Quill bodies are quite easy to wind after one acquires the light touch. I feel it is best not to start tying patterns with this type of body until you have tied several dozen flies. When using peacock eye quill as diagrammed, tie the quill in by its butt end so that the dark side faces the rear of the fly. Be sure the shank of the hook is smooth. Since this quill is not very substantial, many tyers rib it with fine gold or silver wire. You can rib it either clockwise or counterclockwise. The greater strength of wire will help prolong the life of this quill body.

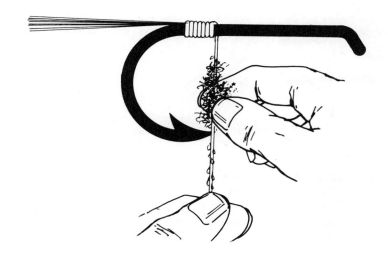

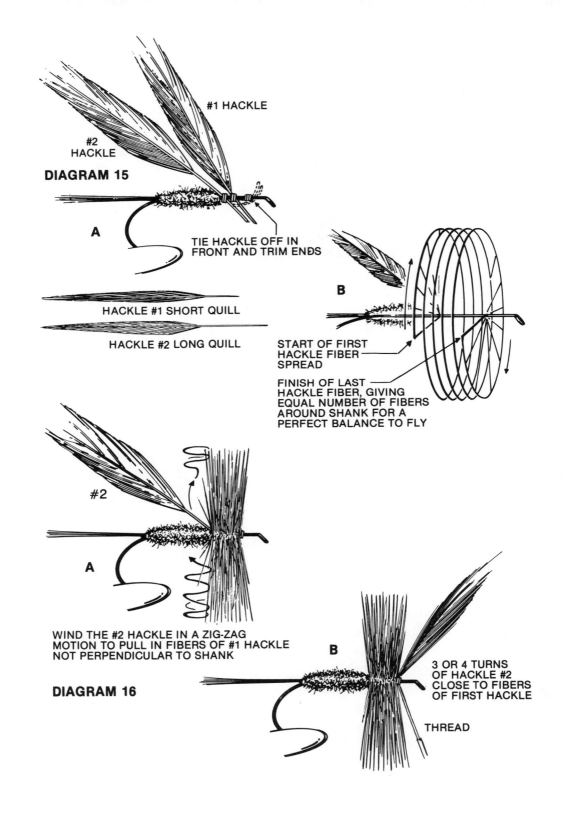

#1 HACKLE

#2 HACKLE

DIAGRAM 15

A

TIE HACKLE OFF IN FRONT AND TRIM ENDS

HACKLE #1 SHORT QUILL

HACKLE #2 LONG QUILL

B

START OF FIRST HACKLE FIBER SPREAD

FINISH OF LAST HACKLE FIBER, GIVING EQUAL NUMBER OF FIBERS AROUND SHANK FOR A PERFECT BALANCE TO FLY

#2

A

WIND THE #2 HACKLE IN A ZIG-ZAG MOTION TO PULL IN FIBERS OF #1 HACKLE NOT PERPENDICULAR TO SHANK

DIAGRAM 16

B

3 OR 4 TURNS OF HACKLE #2 CLOSE TO FIBERS OF FIRST HACKLE

THREAD

10

Tying the Hackle Dry Fly

～～～～～～～

Diagram 15. We are now ready to tie a hackle dry fly. Remember, this dry fly is being constructed so that it will float on the surface of the water. Be careful in the selection of hackle. First of all, the tail material should be from a large hackle (spade or throat hackle) with stiff fibers. Instead of using only a few as you did in the wet fly, tie in enough to hold the hook clear if placed on a flat surface. Next, wind the body as you did in the previous section.

For years I have been asked by many fly tyers how I get the hackle to stand out so perfectly on my dry flies. I have never seen my method described by any other tyer or writer. If you follow the illustrations and procedure you should improve on the quality and beauty of your dry flies.

Select two hackles for the size hook you are tying on. Strip off at least the bottom third. You may have to strip off more if the quill is heavy or stiff; such a hackle is unruly to wind and will twist, and it will be almost impossible to make the fibers stand out perpendicular to the shank of the hook.

When you strip off the webbing, leave one stripped quill long enough to make two or three turns around the shank of the hook. Tie in hackle with the long quill first and then the short quill in front but close to the first hackle. Now bend the stump end of hackle quills to the front and tie down. Do not wind to the eye **(Diagram 15-A)**.

Take hackle number one and wind evenly toward the eye of the hook. Leave enough space behind the eye so you can tie the fly to the leader without tying back the hackle. When you start to wind on the hackle, notice where the fibers start to spread, then try to tie off as close to this point as possible **(Diagram 15-B).** This will give an equal number of fibers around the shank for a perfect balance to the fly.

Diagram 16-A. Now take hackle number two, wind with a zigzag motion behind the first hackle so the stem picks up and binds all hackle fibers of the first hackle that are not standing perpendicular to the shank of the hook. With a slight zigzag, wind up through the first hackle, saving enough for three or four turns in front. Tie off as described for the first hackle. **Diagram 16-B** illustrates this procedure.

Winging techniques are described and illustrated later.

Diagram 17. The *palmer* type dry fly is just a term used to describe the hackle-ribbed body of a fly. Some patterns are tied without, others with wings. Any kind of body can be used.

Before you start tying, let us describe the ribbing hackle. Some tyers always tie in hackle by the tip end and some go so far as to strip fibers from one side. On some hackle the fibers will be progressively longer from the tip to the butt as shown in **Diagram 17-A,** while on others the fibers on the upper two-thirds of the hackle are quite even in length, as in **Diagram 17-B.** To me this variation in fiber length is the determining factor in how I tie in the ribbing hackle. If the hackle is decidedly tapered, tie in by the tip end; however, first hold the hackle by its tip and stroke the fibers down toward the stump end. This will allow you to tie the tip end without having too many fibers tied under.

If I have a relatively even-fibered hackle, I remove the webbing at the stump end and tie in by the stump end. I do not stroke the fibers from this hackle because I believe this stroking may weaken the hackle fiber. In both methods hackles are tied with the dull side out so that the dull side will face the eye when the ribbing is complete. (Note: When tying a palmer wet fly, the top or shiny side of the hackle is out and faces the eye.)

Before starting to tie this fly, carefully study Diagram 17. Note that hackle is now taking the place of tinsel or ribbing, as used in Diagram 11.

Now we are ready for the actual steps. First tie in the tail. Next tie in the ribbing hackle, and the body material last. Wind on body material and tie off one-third the distance in back of the eye. Take hold of the ribbing hackle with your hackle pliers and immediately begin to spiral. As soon as the front end of the body is reached, tie off. The reason for

DIAGRAM 17

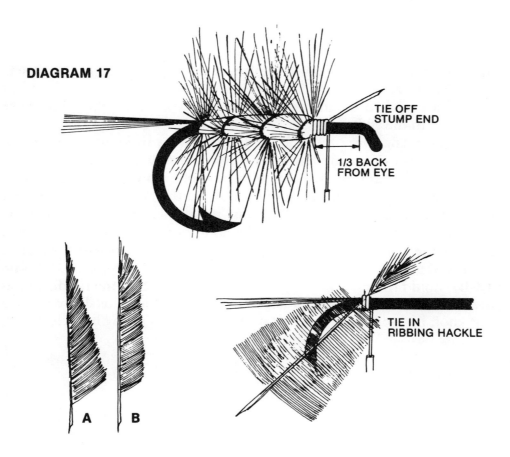

TIE OFF
STUMP END

1/3 BACK
FROM EYE

A   B

TIE IN
RIBBING HACKLE

DIAGRAM 18

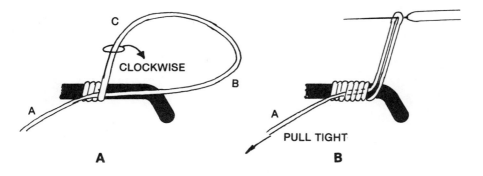

C

CLOCKWISE

A

B

A

A

PULL TIGHT

B

this procedure was thoroughly explained under Diagram 11. Complete your dry fly as described in Diagrams 15 and 16. Be sure the front hackles are tied in so that when they are wound on they will make contact with the ribbing hackle.

Diagram 18. Every tyer should know how to make the whip-finish. After the head of the fly has been formed, throw a half-hitch. Form a loop as in **Diagram 18-A,** holding the top of loop C between the index finger and the thumb of the right hand; hold the bottom B with the left hand. After C has "clamped" B against the shank, let go of B and wind clockwise, using both hands to make additional turns. Each turn must go over the tying thread between A and B. When sufficient turns have been made (four or five), insert dubbing needle in the loop **(Diagram 18-B),** hold firm, and draw tight by pulling at A. Slip the needle out as the knot pulls tight. There is a special tool available to facilitate making this knot, but with practice one can tie it more quickly by hand.

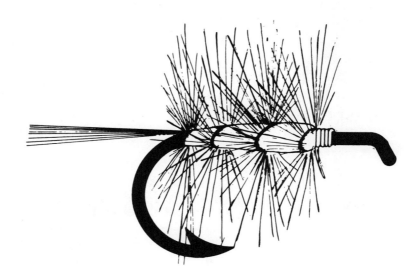

DIAGRAM 19

KEEP ENDS EVEN

CUT OFF HERE

STRIP OFF

BREAST OR FLANK

KEEP ENDS EVEN

CUT OFF HERE

LARGE FLANK OR GRAND NASHUA

CUT OFF HACKLE FIBERS ON TOP

A

DIAGRAM 20

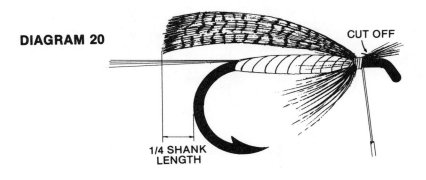

CUT OFF

1/4 SHANK LENGTH

DIAGRAM 21

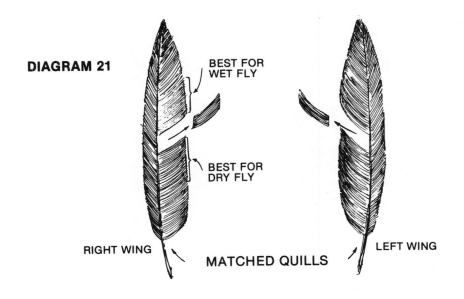

BEST FOR WET FLY

BEST FOR DRY FLY

RIGHT WING

MATCHED QUILLS

LEFT WING

11

The Winged Wet Fly

~~~~~~

MANY fly tyers and fishermen contend that wings are useless and do not add to the fishibility of a fly. I am sorry that I am unable to defend this contention because wings seem to belong on every fly. Most of the flies we fish with today are tied with wings. Bivisibles, hackle flies, spiders, and some palmer flies have no wings. It may be of interest to know that of my many fly-tying acquaintances (and they number in the thousands), the only ones admitting they see no use for wings are those unable to tie a decent fly with wings. I might add that the true artisan would never think of omitting the wings on a pattern that called for them.

Not long ago an elderly man who had been tying flies for many years dropped in to see me about his fly-tying problem. Yes, you have guessed correctly, his trouble was wings. Like all fly tyers, he produced a box containing a sample of his handiwork. His flies were exceptionally well tied in every respect except the wings, which were terrible. When I told him I could remedy all of his troubles in just a few minutes he looked at me, and I believe he thought, "You don't know *me*." Nevertheless, in less than an hour he had mastered a few fundamentals and was tying winged flies as if he had been tying them all his life. When we finished, he turned to me and said, "It really is simple when you know how."

This is true, and any tyer who carefully follows the illustrations and explanations can tie winged flies. Let me caution you to be careful in the selection of the material you use in every fly. Poor material is hard to work with and is very discouraging to the beginner.

The first winged fly I will describe is the easiest to tie. The most common feathers for this type of wing are the breast or flank feathers from various species of duck such as mallard, teal, wood duck, canvasback, and recently, hen saddle feathers.

Diagram 19 illustrates how to prepare the feathers and where to cut the sections to be used. First of all, tie a common hackle wet fly. In case there is any question in your mind about this fly, review Diagrams 7 to 10. Let me remind the tyer that the body should be slightly tapered toward the head of the fly. A body that is too heavy at the front end will tend to make the wings stand up too high. Be sure you do not run the hackle up close to the eye of the hook or there will not be room to tie on the wings and it will be impossible to properly finish off the fly. When the hackle is secured, better throw on one half-hitch so that, if the wing slips or must be removed for another try, the hackle will not come unwound. With the preceding points in mind you are ready to begin.

Take your scissors and cut off the hackle fibers on top of the fly (**Diagram 19-A**). This cutting is optional but seems to make a neater fly. Take breast or flank feathers and strip off the downy area at the bottom. Continue stripping from the stump end upward until the fibers are uniform in quality and as near the same length as possible in the area you are going to use. Keep the ends of these fibers even. Cut out a section and roll or fold together so the fibers are all in one bunch.

Diagram 20 shows wet-fly proportions and how to hold the wings. Hold by the butt end using the thumb and index fingers of your right hand. Lay along the top of the hook so you can see how far the wings will extend beyond the hook. Now trade hands and tie in close up against the hackle using the same procedure as was used to tie on the tail (see Diagrams 4 and 23). As soon as the wing is secured with several turns, cut off as shown. Make enough turns to cover up material and finish off in the usual manner.

Diagram 21. Wing quills are most frequently used for the wings of wet flies. Many species of bird have suitable quills. Duck-wing quills are more commonly used than any other; they are best for the beginner to practice with because the fibers hold together quite well. Study Diagram 21 and notice that the center half of the quill is usually the best. Select two matched quills. By this I mean one quill from the left and one from the right wing. They should be as near the same size and conformity as possible. Now cut a section from each quill about three-fourths as wide as the gap of the hook you are tying on. The tendency for the beginner

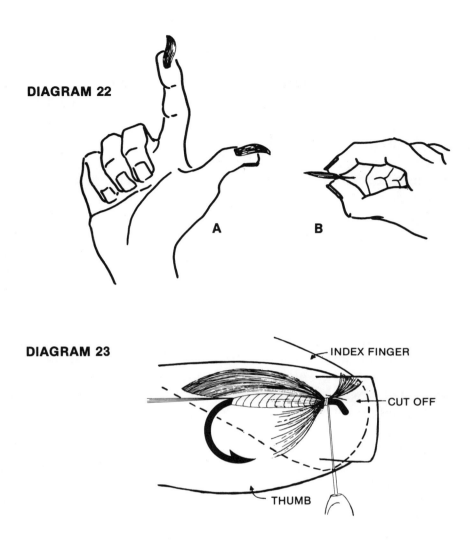

DIAGRAM 22

A B

DIAGRAM 23

INDEX FINGER

CUT OFF

THUMB

is to use wings that are too wide. Place the wings so that the concave surfaces are facing each other.

Diagram 22. This diagram illustrates one method of placing the wings together. I believe it is the easiest and quickest way for anyone to get the two wings together. Moisten the thumb and index finger of the right hand. Notice the angle at which they adhere to the thumb and finger in **Diagram 22-A.** This angle is right for me but may not be for you if your finger and thumb differ from mine in angle of grasp. Experiment until you find the correct angle. When the thumb and finger are closed, as in **Diagram 22-B,** the tips of the wing section should match and the sides should be even.

If you have placed the wing sections on the thumb and finger as in Diagram 22, the contour of the fibers will be down. The wings may be tied on in this manner or reversed so that the tip ends point upward. If they are pointed up, hold them by the cut ends in the right hand and gently stroke the tip ends downward with the left. This gives your wings a nice rounded end.

Diagram 23. This is the closed-wing wet fly. Hold the wings between the thumb and forefinger of the left hand. Check the diagram carefully for the correct position. Note that the thumb and forefinger straddle the shank of the hook and that the wings are laid down to come in contact with the top of the body. The tips of the thumb and finger, when closed, should extend to (or slightly beyond) the eye of the hook. All other operations are the same as described in Diagram 4. Hold the wings firmly until they are secured. Once you have made a turn or two around the wing, never make another turn back of the first one toward the bend. If you do, this will turn, fold, or split the wings. The technique just described is one of the most important in fly tying. Once you have mastered it, you will never have trouble setting any kind of wing.

Diagram 24. This diagram illustrates how one section from either a right or left quill may be formed to make the wings for a wet fly. This technique is seldom used by the average tyer, but is quite simple once it is mastered. In this diagram we are working with a section from the quill of a right wing. Cut section, (**Diagram 24-A**), and hold firmly in both hands as illustrated. Now move your hands slightly in the opposite direction. Next, hold firmly by the cut end (left hand) and gently stroke the tip ends upward between the thumb and forefinger of the right hand. Reverse the operation by holding the tip with the right hand and stroking in the opposite direction with the left. Repeat this operation until the tip ends are even, as in **Diagram 24-B.** Fold section longitudinally in the middle. Follow procedure under Diagram 23 to finish. Only use this method if you do not have matched wing quills.

DIAGRAM 24

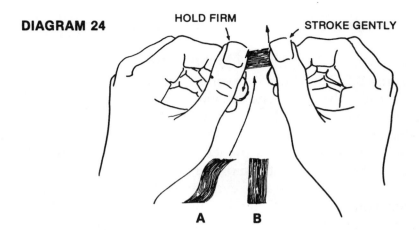

HOLD FIRM

STROKE GENTLY

A   B

DIAGRAM 25

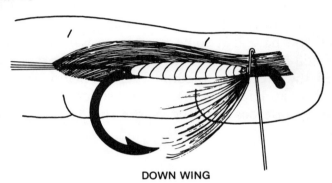

DOWN WING

DIAGRAM 26

The Down-Wing

Diagrams 25, 26. The down-wing is quite often troublesome for the beginner. After the body and hackling are finished, cut off the hackle fibers along both sides. (This is optional.) Take the wing for the left side as in Diagram 25 and place it on the far side of your hook. Hold it in place with the index finger of the left hand. The lower edge of the wing should come just to the bottom of the body. Take the wing for the right side and place it opposite and even with the one on the left. Hold in place with your thumb. (Note: For illustrative purposes the right wing has been omitted; for its position see Diagram 26.) Bring the tying thread up loosely between your thumb and the wing, over the top of the wing, and down between the left wing and index finger, then up again between the thumb and right wing. Close the tips of your thumb and finger. Hold firmly and tighten by pulling the thread up as in Diagram 26. After you have had some experience with this wing you may find that you will be able to tie it in as described for the closed wing. I only suggested the preceding method because beginners usually have more success using it. There are many other styles of wings, but if the novice can tie just those described he or she should have no trouble with the other types.

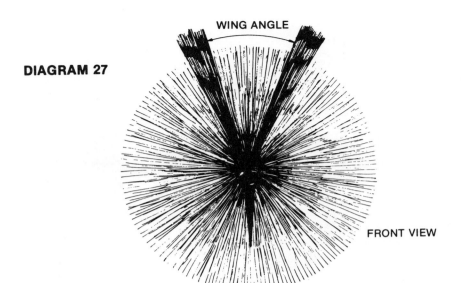

DIAGRAM 27

WING ANGLE

FRONT VIEW

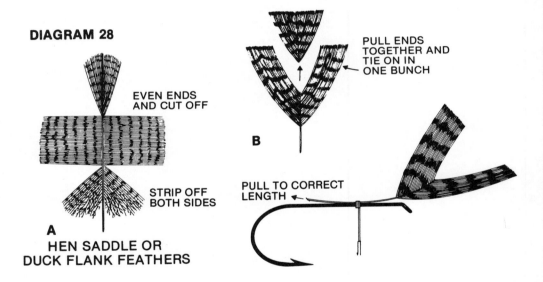

DIAGRAM 28

EVEN ENDS AND CUT OFF

PULL ENDS TOGETHER AND TIE ON IN ONE BUNCH

B

STRIP OFF BOTH SIDES

A
HEN SADDLE OR DUCK FLANK FEATHERS

PULL TO CORRECT LENGTH

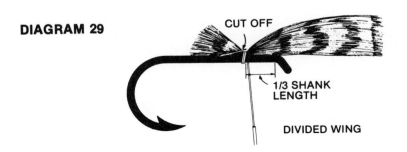

DIAGRAM 29

CUT OFF

1/3 SHANK LENGTH

DIVIDED WING

12

The Winged Dry Fly

~~~~~~~~~~

THE winged dry fly is tied so that it will float on the surface of the water. However, it is supposed to float with the wings in an upright or spentwing position, depending of course on how it was originally constructed. With the winged dry fly the tyer must pay more attention to detail than with any other type of fly. For the standard fly tied on regular-shank hooks, the hackle should be sized carefully. The wings usually give the beginner the most trouble. Remember, it is better to have the wings a little short than too long. Wings that are too long will make the fly top heavy and it will have a tendency to spin and twist the leader during casting and will not ride the water as it should. The tail should be as long as the shank of the hook (except when using short- or long-shanked hooks), and stiff enough, along with the hackle, to support the fly. The body of the fly should be slim rather than heavy.

Always keep in mind that no matter how well dressed the fly may be, it is no better than the material used to construct it. Always use the best material available and continually strive for perfection.

Diagram 27. This diagram illustrates the approximate length and angle to cock the upright wings on a dry fly. It would be well for the neophyte tyer to study the diagram and imitate the angle as closely as possible. One should realize that there may be considerable variance with each hook size insofar as the length of the wing is concerned because the wing is usually about one-fourth longer than the hackle.

Diagram 28. This diagram illustrates the most common methods of preparing breast, side, or flank feathers of various ducks and hen saddle feathers for the divided wing. First select a feather that is well marked and of uniform quality. Strip off all the soft and downy fibers. If the feather is large, sections may be cut from either side as shown in **Diagram 28-A** and placed together so that the ends are even. Sometimes you may be able to get enough from one side of the feather for the wings, thus eliminating cutting from each side. When the feathers are small and you only have enough fibers to make one pair of wings, the best method is to cut out the center as illustrated in **Diagram 28-B.** The length of the wings determines how far back to cut out the center section.

With a feather as in Diagram 28-B, I usually tie in the quill with two turns of tying thread (**Diagram 28-C**) then pull the quill until the fibers of the feathers are the correct length for the wings. Proceed as illustrated.

Diagram 29. For a divided-wing dry fly, first attach tying thread to the hook and wind up to one-fourth the distance back of the eye. When the wings are tied in on this base it helps keep the wings from turning. Wind thread back to the center of the shank and tie in the tail. Be sure to tie enough tail fibers to support the weight of the fly. Now wind back to one-third the distance in back of the eye. You are now ready to set the wings. If the sections cut from the side of the feather are used, be sure the ends of the fibers are even. Roll or fold together and hold in a compact bunch between the thumb and forefinger of the left hand, with the tip ends on the outside. The fibers are held in a position opposite from the way they are held when tying in the tail. The solid bunch of fibers is tied in approximately one-third the distance back of the eye, using the same technique as described in Diagram 23. Remember, the wings should be about one-fourth longer than the fibers of the hackle on this fly. Make enough turns to hold the fibers fast, then cut off the excess on an angle, as illustrated.

Diagram 30 illustrates the next step. Grasp wing material and pull to an upright position; wind tying thread in front of the wings. Make enough turns tight in against the base to form a wedge that will hold the wing material perpendicular to the shank of the hook.

Diagram 31. Use both hands and separate the fibers into even bunches. The tying thread is now at the position labeled "start," as shown in **Diagram 31-A.** Hold the wing on the left side and wind the thread back between the wings, crossing to the other side. Let the wing on the left go and grasp the wing on the right side, winding the thread

DIAGRAM 30

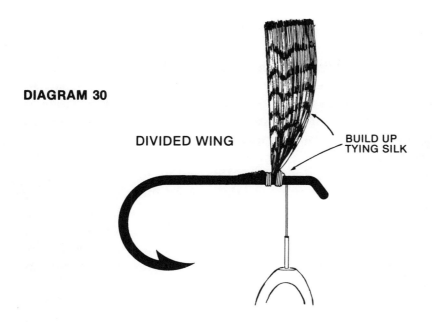

DIVIDED WING

BUILD UP
TYING SILK

DIAGRAM 31

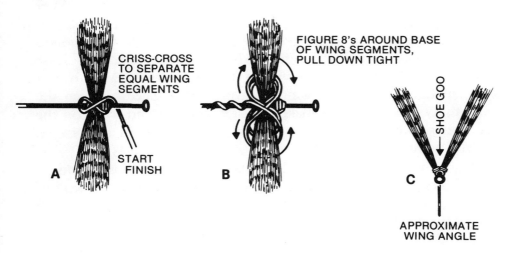

CRISS-CROSS
TO SEPARATE
EQUAL WING
SEGMENTS

START
FINISH

A

FIGURE 8's AROUND BASE
OF WING SEGMENTS,
PULL DOWN TIGHT

B

SHOE GOO

C

APPROXIMATE
WING ANGLE

in under the shank at the rear of the wings. Now bring your thread forward and across to the front of the wings and then under the shank to a point near your starting position, marked "finish." Cock the wings as illustrated in Diagram 27, and repeat winding this crisscross pattern until the wings cock at the desired angle. Usually two or three turns are sufficient. After the necessary crisscrosses have been made, end with the thread in front of the wings, as in "start." Proceeding to **Diagram 31-B,** grasp the wing on the left side with the thumb and index finger of your left hand and cross the thread to the left, backward to the rear of the right wing. Release the left wing and grasp the right wing. Bring the thread forward around the base of the right wing, then up and across on top of the shank, going back between the wings to the rear of the left wing. Release the right wing and grasp the left wing and wind the thread forward around the base of the left wing. Now bring the thread up and, crossing over, take it back between the wings. Next, carefully spiral the thread back along the shank of the hook. If too much tension is applied during this last operation, the thread will bend the wings and slip off, or will pull them too close together. When you finish, the wings should be cocked approximately as illustrated in **Diagram 31-C.** Put a small drop of Shoe Goo between the wings to hold them fast. After several pairs of wings have been set, the beginning tyer is usually able to judge the correct tension for this operation. Hairwings are attached using the same procedure. Use Diagram 31-A for spentwings.

The body is next. Since this is a winged fly it is a good idea not to run the body up tight against the wing. Leave a small space between the body and the wings. This will make it easier to tie in and wind on the hackles. This procedure should be strictly observed when dubbing is used for the body.

Now tie in both hackles and follow instructions and illustrations in Diagrams 15 and 16. You should now be able to finish off the head of the fly with a whip-finish. A small drop of cement should be applied to the head of the fly. *Finis!*

Quill-Section Wings

The quill-section winged dry fly is gradually losing its popularity simply because it is not very durable. The spent hen saddle and hairwinged flies

DIAGRAM 32

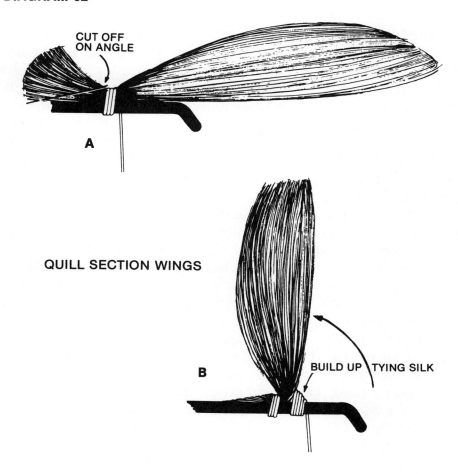

CUT OFF
ON ANGLE

A

QUILL SECTION WINGS

B

BUILD UP TYING SILK

are slowly creeping in, and I believe you will eventually see them replace the quill-section wings.

Diagrams 32A and **B** illustrate how this type of wing is set. This operation should not be too difficult because many of the procedures are quite similar to the setting of quill wings on the wet fly.

Secure the tying thread and wind up to one-third the distance in back of the eye. Cut wing sections. It is best to take these sections from the lower part of the quills where the curvature is more pronounced. Lay the sections together so their convex sides are against one another. Tie in as illustrated in Diagram 32-A, one-third the distance in back of the eye. There is one important detail to remember: When you grasp the sections between the thumb and index finger of the left hand, grasp them in such a way that when they are held on top of the hook and the thumb and finger are squeezed together prior to tightening up the thread, the ends of the thumb and finger are at least up to, or extend slightly over, the eye of the hook. This procedure prevents separation and roll of wing fibers. As soon as the wings are secured, cut off any excess stump end. Next, grasp the wings firmly as close to the hook as possible and pull to an upright position.

Now build up a wedge of tying thread in front to hold the wings in a perpendicular position. If the wings need to be separated, make a very loose crisscross pattern. Grasp the base of the wing between the thumb and index finger of the left hand and squeeze gently, using about the same pressure as you used when the wing was originally tied on. Tighten up the crisscross and then spiral the thread backward on the shank. Finish the fly as described in previous illustrations.

Diagram 33. This diagram illustrates the way breast feathers are prepared for the fanwing flies. Carefully match a pair of breast feathers and strip off down to the point where the wings are the correct size for the fly you are tying. Do not cut off the quill.

Diagram 34. Your tying thread should be one-third the distance in back of the eye. Grasp the wings in your left hand so that the convex sides are together. Hold the wings on the hook so that the stems straddle the shank, allowing a little of the bared stem to protrude above the shank. Make enough turns to secure the stems, as in **Diagram 34-A.** Hold the wings tightly while making additional turns around the stems above the shank sufficient to bind them securely together.

Diagram 34-B. Brace the wings by winding the thread down and around the shank, as in **Diagram 34-C.** Be sure the wings are not cocked to the right or left but are in perfect alignment with the longitudinal plane of the shank of the hook. In order to correct misalignment in the event the wings are cocked to the right, take a turn or two clockwise around the base of the wings. Next bring the thread down and under the shank in front of the wings, applying enough tension to pull the wings into proper alignment. If the wings are cocked to the left, reverse this procedure. When the wings are perfectly

DIAGRAM 33

BREAST FEATHER

STRIP OFF

FAN WING

DIAGRAM 34

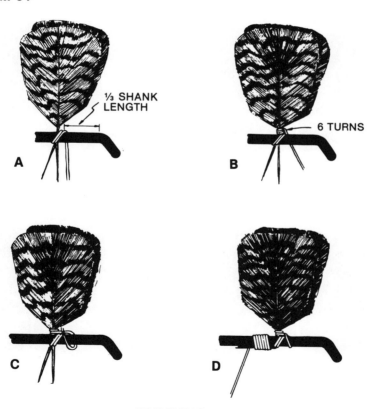

⅓ SHANK LENGTH

A

6 TURNS

B

C

D

FAN WING

balanced, pull the stems up and tie them fast to the shank, as in **Diagram 34-D.** Finish the fly in the usual manner.

I know of no greater crime than to pick up a beautiful dry fly and, by mishandling, crush the hackle or wings. The fruit of a half-hour's labor can be ruined in just a second or two by such an act. I have heard many fishermen say an old "beat-up" dry fly is best! I am ready to admit I have taken many trout on flies in this condition, but I know from experience that a well-dressed dry fly with good-quality hackle, one that will ride the water as it was meant to do, will consistently take more trout. Keep this in mind during all steps when tying the dry fly.

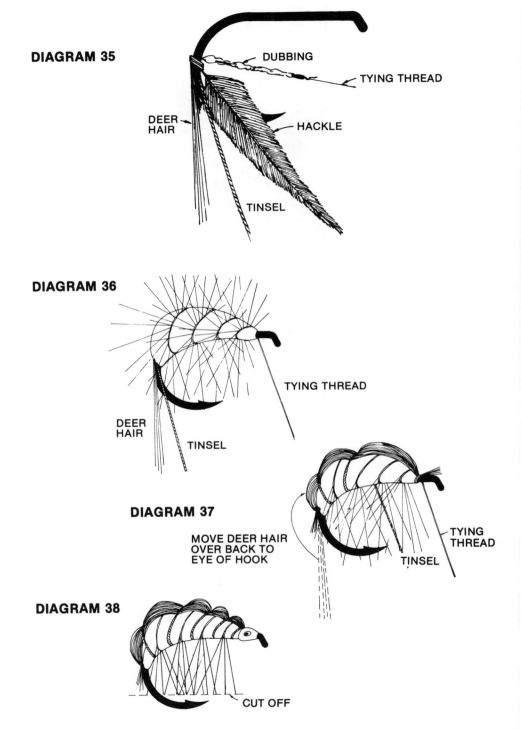

DIAGRAM 35

DUBBING

TYING THREAD

DEER HAIR

HACKLE

TINSEL

DIAGRAM 36

TYING THREAD

DEER HAIR

TINSEL

DIAGRAM 37

MOVE DEER HAIR OVER BACK TO EYE OF HOOK

TYING THREAD

TINSEL

DIAGRAM 38

CUT OFF

13

The Shrimp Fly

~~~~~~~~

Diagram 35. The shrimp fly is very effective in both fresh and salt water. Many fly tyers for some reason have difficulty tying an acceptable imitation. The following illustrations and descriptions should solve the problem. It is best to use a short-shank hook and start tying material in down on the bend of the hook, as illustrated.

Materials should be tied on in the following sequence:

1. Tail (optional)
2. Deer tail hair or any other hair may be used if it is long enough and the right color. This may be dyed or natural depending on your selection of color combinations.
3. Tinsel or fine wire
4. Ribbing hackle
5. Dubbing. This is spun on tying thread as illustrated in Diagram 13.

Diagrams 36, 37, 38. The dubbed body should be built up to the desired shape. It is usually tapered slightly from rear to front and heavier than a regular wet-fly body. When the body is completed, the tying thread should be in back of the eye as illustrated. Spiral the ribbing hackle to the front of the body and tie off as shown in Diagram 36. As each spiral is made, stroke the hackle fibers down toward the belly of the fly. Now cut off the hackle fibers from the top and those sticking out at the sides. Most fibers should be on the bottom, as shown in Diagram 37. The deer hair is now twisted, held firmly, and pulled up over the back to the front of the body and tied off. The ribbing material (tinsel or wire) is spiraled over and tied off as illustrated in Diagram 38. Personally, I wind either the hackle or ribbing material counterclockwise. This secures the hackle. Finally, build up the head with tying thread. Lacquer, enamel (usually several coats), and put on the eyes. The easiest way to fix the eyes is to take two round toothpicks and cut off the ends so that one is of greater diameter than the other. Dip the end of the larger in the selected enamel (just a drop) and press lightly on the side of the head until the desired diameter of iris is obtained. Do the same on the other side. Allow plenty of time to dry. Next, dip the smaller-diameter toothpick in the second color of enamel and superimpose the pupil in the center of the iris of both eyes. After drying thoroughly, apply several coats of clear cement. Trim off the hackle as illustrated in Diagram 38.

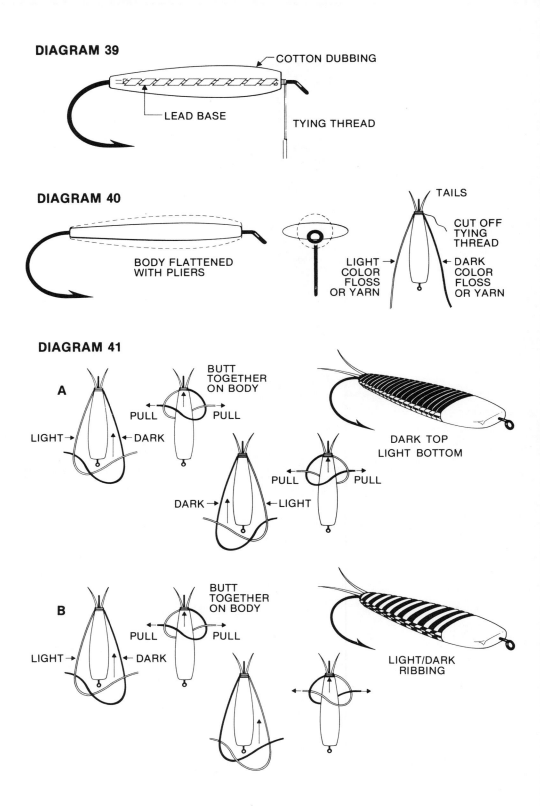

DIAGRAM 39

COTTON DUBBING

LEAD BASE

TYING THREAD

DIAGRAM 40

BODY FLATTENED
WITH PLIERS

TAILS

CUT OFF
TYING
THREAD

LIGHT
COLOR
FLOSS
OR YARN

DARK
COLOR
FLOSS
OR YARN

DIAGRAM 41

A

BUTT
TOGETHER
ON BODY

PULL   PULL

LIGHT →   ← DARK

DARK →   ← LIGHT

PULL   PULL

DARK TOP
LIGHT BOTTOM

B

BUTT
TOGETHER
ON BODY

PULL   PULL

LIGHT →   ← DARK

LIGHT/DARK
RIBBING

14
Woven Nymphs

ANYONE who can tie a common wet or dry fly should have no trouble tying nymphs. Most are quite simple to tie, and if one sees a pattern, he should be able to duplicate it providing he has the materials used in its construction. There is one exception, the woven-bodied nymphs. Two methods will be illustrated and described. Some nymphs are tied so they will float or ride the surface film. These of course need no weight. When I tie weighted nymphs I indicate the amount of weight by the color of the head. A lightly weighted nymph has a yellow head, a medium-weighted one has an orange head, a heavy one a black head, and one with no weight a white head. This is important because different weighted nymphs are needed to fish all types of water. Any color scheme is satisfactory as long as you know what color represents each weight.

Diagrams 39, 40. If the nymph is to be weighted, cover the shank of the hook with Super Glue, available at any supermarket or hardware store. Now tightly wind on the lead wire; the glue will keep the lead from slipping. To end with a slender-bodied nymph, cover the lead by winding tying thread over the lead base until the body is smooth and of the desired shape. Apply Shoe Goo or lacquer and put aside until dry. I usually prepare a dozen or so bodies before I start working on the finished product. For a larger, flattened body, after securing the lead base, dub surgical cotton on the tying thread and build up the body to the desired diameter and tie off as in Diagram 39. Apply a coat of quick-drying cement and when it is almost dry, flatten the body by squeezing with pliers as illustrated in Diagram 40. This is the base for the woven-bodied stonefly.

Now tie in the tail. This may be stripped hackle or short fibers from wing quills. Next tie in two colors of floss or yarn, dark on the right side, light on the left side. Half-hitch, then cut off the tying thread.

Clayton Peters originated this method. Turn the vise so the eye of the hook faces you. Tie an overhand knot with the dark strand coming under, then over, the light strand. Open the loop so that the dark strand is on top and slip back over the body to the tail.

Diagram 41-A. Draw the knot up tight by pulling both dark and light floss horizontally in opposite directions. The dark strand will now be on the left. Always tie the knot so the dark strand comes under the light strand. Keep repeating until you have the body woven about three-quarters of the way up the shank toward the eye. Attach the thread and tie off the body.

If you want a ribbed body as in **Diagram 41-B,** start with the dark strand coming under, then over, the light strand. On the next knot, bring the light strand coming under, then over, the dark strand. This will give alternating light and dark ribbing.

Diagrams 42, 43, 44. Take a section of prepared turkey wing quill, about as wide as the nymph body. (To prepare, give the quill a coat of Shoe Goo solution and allow to dry.) Tie in this section over the front end of the body (Diagram 42). Now spin yellowish olive dubbing (mixed dyed rabbit) on tying thread and wind to form the back of the thorax. Tie in a small bunch of partridge or hen saddle fibers on each side for legs (Diagram 43). If you want to have separate legs you may tie or cement in three short duck quill fibers on each side. In both cases you spin dubbing on tying thread and wind between legs or in front and back of bunches of fibers so you will give the thorax a solid covering of dubbing (Diagram 44). You now should have the tying thread in front of the thorax. Pull the turkey section up front, hold firmly, and take four or five turns of the tying thread around the feather in front of the thorax. This represents the wing pad.

Take a piece of thirty-pound test nylon a little longer than eye spacing, and touch the ends with a flame from a cigarette lighter. This will form small round balls for eyes. Lay across the turkey feather and double back the feather. Tie off behind the nylon eyes (**Diagram 44-A**).

Bead chain of gold or silver makes unique eyes. Tie bead-chain eyes in after the legs, then finish as described for nylon eyes. Cover all exposed tying thread with Shoe Goo solution.

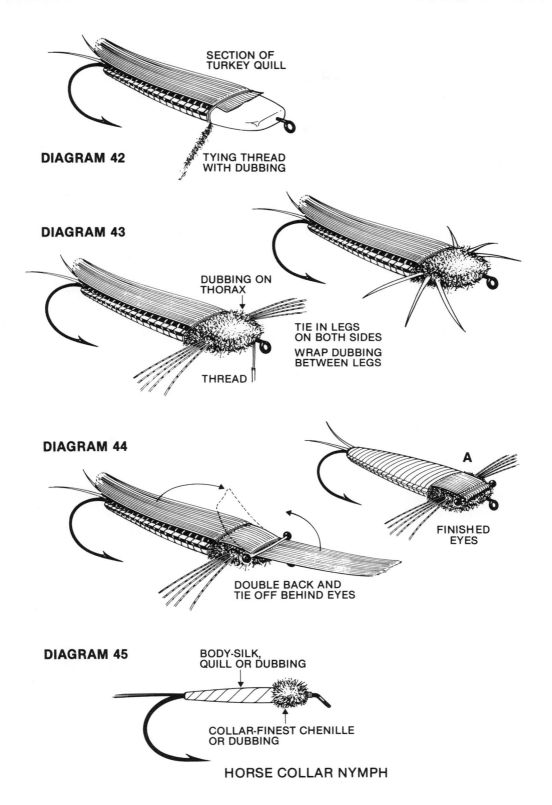

DIAGRAM 42

SECTION OF
TURKEY QUILL

TYING THREAD
WITH DUBBING

DIAGRAM 43

DUBBING ON
THORAX

TIE IN LEGS
ON BOTH SIDES

WRAP DUBBING
BETWEEN LEGS

THREAD

DIAGRAM 44

A

FINISHED
EYES

DOUBLE BACK AND
TIE OFF BEHIND EYES

DIAGRAM 45

BODY-SILK,
QUILL OR DUBBING

COLLAR-FINEST CHENILLE
OR DUBBING

HORSE COLLAR NYMPH

Diagram 45 shows the Horse Collar Nymph. Tie in a few fibers for the tail. The body should be quill, silk floss, or dubbing. The collar is of chenille or dubbing and should match the body color. This nymph is so easy to tie that no description is necessary.

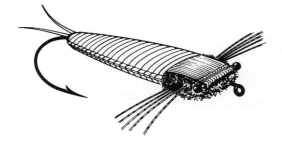

DIAGRAM 46

STRIP LEAD

WEIGHTED BODIES

DIAGRAM 47

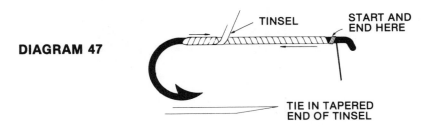

TINSEL

START AND
END HERE

TIE IN TAPERED
END OF TINSEL

DIAGRAM 48

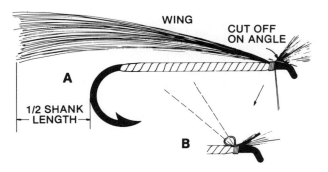

WING

CUT OFF
ON ANGLE

A

1/2 SHANK
LENGTH

B

DIAGRAM 49

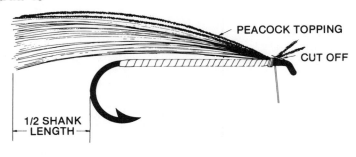

PEACOCK TOPPING

CUT OFF

1/2 SHANK
LENGTH

15

The Streamer Fly

～～～～～～

THE feather- and hairwinged streamer flies are probably the most interesting for the beginner to tie. Many patterns are quite gaudy in color, some really eye-catching in their beauty. Practically every conceivable combination of feathers and hair has been used to construct these flies and the beginner can experiment at will. Strange as it may seem to some, it will be practically impossible to tie up any creations that will not take fish.

Some fly tyers believe it is best to start the beginner tying the larger bucktails and streamers. I have tried various sequences and have found the students in my classes tied better and neater flies by following the procedures described in this book. My students have ranged in age from three years to seventy.

Streamer flies are normally tied on long-shank hooks. Since these flies are usually regarded as a forage fish, the length of the wings on the same pattern may vary considerably from one location to another. Of course there are many fancy and·highly colored patterns that do not imitate anything and are no doubt taken by the fish simply out of curiosity. These should be called *attractor* flies. The streamer flies are by far the most versatile type of fly known today because any fish that will take any artificial lure can be caught on a streamer fly. This not only applies to freshwater fish but to saltwater species as well.

These flies are effective because of the undulating action they produce when wet. It is well for the beginner to keep this in mind because if the fly is dressed too heavily, such action is lost. This loss of action is especially true with hairwinged streamers.

The most common problem encountered when tying feather-wing

127

streamers (particularly when using saddle hackle) is matching the hackle. Following is the procedure I use when tying more than several flies:

1. Select hackles that are as nearly uniform as possible.
2. Soak the hackle in a pan of water until the quills are soft and pliable.
3. On a dry pane of glass, hold each hackle by pressing down on the stump with the index finger of the left hand. With the right thumb, stroke the hackle in a straight line from the stump to the tip end. Set aside until the hackle is completely dry. When dry, put in a box (I use a cigar box) and shake vigorously until the feathers fluff out and are normal looking. Your hackle will now be straight and easily matched.

Diagram 46. Many streamer flies are tied with or without weighted bodies. For weighted bodies, strip lead is generally conceded to be the best because it is flat and easy to work with. If strip lead is not available, use lead wires. Any weighting material that is not flat makes the winding of smooth, ridgeless tinsel bodies difficult. Lead may be purchased in sheets and cut into various widths suitable to the hook's size. The lead may be wrapped compactly or slightly spaced, as in Diagram 46. The spacing depends upon the weight you desire to have in the finished fly. The lead may be wrapped on in precisely the same manner used in the building of bodies previously described. I prefer to spin on the strip lead and so will describe this method. I feel it is the quickest and best.

Grasp the end of the lead between the thumb and index finger of your right hand and hold tightly a bit farther back with the left hand. Twist the end in your right hand one or two turns counterclockwise around the shank of the hook just in back of the eye. Now the lead is started. Keep feeding the lead with the left hand while spinning counterclockwise with the right until you have the shank of the hook covered as in Diagram 46. Do not run the lead all the way back to the bend or up close to the eye. Secure the tying thread in back of the eye, then take a few turns over the first turn of lead to secure the lead and keep it from spinning when the body is wrapped over it. All bodies, with the exception of tinsel bodies, are tied and wrapped on in the usual manner.

Diagram 47 illustrates the technique used in winding on the tinsel body. First, cut one end of the tinsel to a tapered point. This end is tied in at the point marked "start" in this diagram. This tapered end makes it much easier to start winding in the tinsel smoothly. Just to convince yourself, try tying in tinsel with a square end and see how it is nearly impossible to start winding tinsel without causing a hump. Wind the tinsel clockwise and close together over the lead base up to the bend of the hook. Return as diagrammed to the starting point and tie off in the usual manner. If the tyer is going to tie several flies of the same pattern, it will save time if he ties all the bodies first. This is the procedure most professional tyers use; of course, they may tie several hundred dozen of the same pattern.

Diagram 48. This diagram illustrates the method of tying on the hairwing or bucktail-type streamer fly. It is rather difficult to suggest an exact length for the streamer wing because in different localities the length of the wing varies. I believe the most popular length is about one and one-half times as long as the shank of the hook.

Cut a section of hair near the roots and hold by their tip ends in the left hand. With the right hand pull out all short hairs and fur. Now hold by the butt end and pull out all the long hairs. Next, put back a bunch so as to keep the tip ends as even as possible. If you are not sure of the amount of hair to use for this wing, I suggest you purchase a hairwing streamer fly to use as a model. Hold the hair in the same manner as was shown for the tail and tie in as illustrated. After the wing is secured, cut off any excess on an angle, as in **Diagram 48-A.** Hold the wing up and wind your tying thread around the base, as in **Diagram 48-B.** Continue making several more turns over the wings in the usual manner.

Diagram 49. Topping is used on some hairwing patterns. Quite often this may be peacock herl or golden-pheasant crest feathers, but many others may be used depending entirely on the pattern. Tie in as illustrated in this diagram and cut off the excess.

Diagram 50. The throat on the streamer fly is usually fibers from a large hackle but fibers from many other feathers are used depending on the pattern. The length of the throat varies, but usually does not extend beyond the point of the hook. It will probably be easier for the beginner to take the hook out of the vise and turn the bottom side up before tying in the throat. It may be tied in by the same method as the tail.

The experienced tyer never changes the hook but holds the material under the shank and ties it from the bottom. First, select material and cut to the desired length. Straddle the shank of the hook with the thumb and index finger of the left hand. Pick up the throat material with the right hand and transfer it to the thumb and index finger of the left hand so that the tip ends of the fibers point toward the rear of the hook and the stump end is positioned where it should be tied in (right below the wing). Bring the tying thread down between your finger and the throat material, then up on the opposite side between the thumb and throat. Squeeze thumb and finger together and tighten by pulling up. This is just the reverse of the procedure used to tie in the tail.

Diagram 51. The shoulder, cheek, or eye are all tied on in the same manner. Select two feathers with identical markings and as near the same size and shape as possible. Strip off fibers until the feathers are the desired size. Do not cut the quill or mid-rib. Hold on the side, securing the quill at the point where the fibers start, and tie in with several turns of the tying thread. Now, take hold of the mid-rib and gently pull the feathers into the desired position as illustrated in this diagram. It is a good idea to pull the shoulder feather far enough so that a few of the fibers are just under the tying thread. This will help keep the shoulder from turning or twisting out of position. Follow this same procedure for the other shoulder. Cut off any excess stumps and complete by winding on enough tying thread to cover all visible material and to give a nice smooth head. Finish in the usual manner and cement the head any desired color.

Diagram 52. The feather-wing streamer is one of the most popular and best fish-takers of all streamer flies. I believe the angler can more closely imitate many of the natural minnows with this type of fly because of the wide variety of feathers and numerous colored hackles one has to choose from. In addition, the undulating action produced by the saddle hackle is very lifelike and as a result presents a very tempting lure for the fish.

Saddle hackles—the long, tapering, fine, quilled or mid-ribbed hackle that hang down on the flank of a mature cock bird—are the best feathers for this type of fly. If none are available, the large neck hackles may be substituted. I would recommend, when using the neck hackle, that you select necks that have slender quilled hackles if possible. The heavy quilled hackles do not have nearly the undulating action when fished and are harder to work with.

First build up the body, then select matching hackle for wings. I usually use four hackles, two for each side, with the concave sides facing

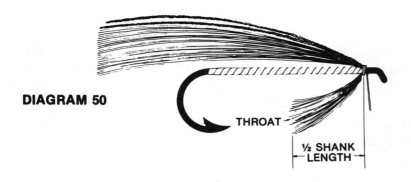

DIAGRAM 50

THROAT

½ SHANK
LENGTH

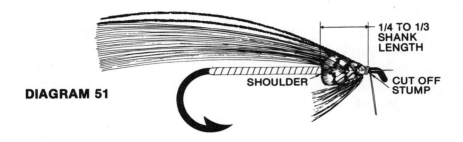

DIAGRAM 51

SHOULDER

1/4 TO 1/3
SHANK
LENGTH

CUT OFF
STUMP

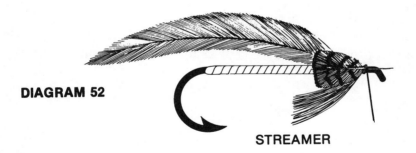

DIAGRAM 52

STREAMER

DIAGRAM 53

COMBINATION BUCKTAIL AND STREAMER

1. BODY
2. TINSEL OR RIBBING
3. WING
4. TOPPING
5. BELLY
6. THROAT
7. SHOULDER
8. EYE

3   4   8

GRAY GHOST

1   2   5   6   7

ORDER IN WHICH MATERIAL IS TIED ON

each other. Be sure you have the ends even. Strip off excess fibers from the stump end until you have the desired length. Hold in exactly the same manner as when tying in the tail. All other steps are as previously described.

Diagram 53. This diagram shows the order in which materials are tied on for a combination bucktail and feather-wing streamer. I will describe the Gray Ghost, with red throat added.

Body: Orange silk floss ribbed with gold tinsel

Wing: Four slate gray or blue dun matched saddle hackles

Topping: Golden pheasant crest feathers.

Belly: Four strands of peacock herl are tied in first, then white and yellow bucktail

Throat: Red hackle fibers (added for illustrative purposes only)

Shoulder: Silver or zebra pheasant-breast feathers

Eye: Jungle cock neck feathers

Belly is a term I use that is new to the fly-tying trade. I use it whenever any material is tied on the underside of a streamer that represents the belly of a minnow and is approximately as long as the wing. The term commonly used to describe this, *throat,* is not an adequate term because both "throat" and "belly" may be used on the same fly. The throat is really a beard-type hackle, rarely extending beyond the point of the hook.

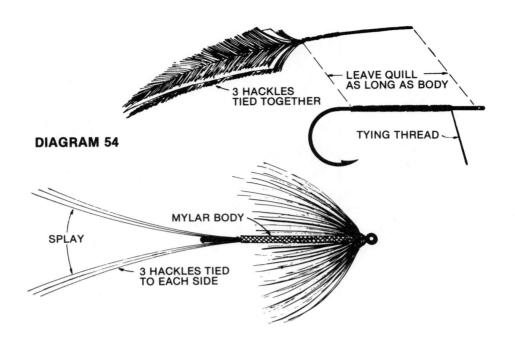

3 HACKLES
TIED TOGETHER

LEAVE QUILL
AS LONG AS BODY

TYING THREAD

DIAGRAM 54

MYLAR BODY

SPLAY

3 HACKLES TIED
TO EACH SIDE

DIAGRAM 55

HACKLED FEATHER WING STREAMER

DIAGRAM 56

BUCKTAIL

TINSEL BODY

16

Saltwater Flies

~~~~~~~~~~

SALTWATER flies generally have wings that are much longer than their freshwater counterparts. Because of this some changes in construction are called for. If you tie the longer-wing saltwater flies with the wings tied in at the head, the wings will be separating and catching in the bend of the hook. When this occurs the fly will not fish correctly and will not take fish consistently. The freshwater method may only be used on small saltwater flies.

In the following diagrams weighted bodies will not be illustrated because they were covered for freshwater flies (Diagram 46).

Most saltwater flies are tied on noncorrosive hooks. If freshwater hooks are used they will quickly corrode and rust unless washed in fresh water each time they have been used in salt water.

Diagram 54. Any hair that is long enough may be used for the hairwinged flies; bucktail is the most commonly used. Before tying in hair or feather wings, cover the shank of the hook with tying thread, ending up in back of the eye. If the wing material is long enough, tie it in back of the eye where the body would normally end. Now wind your thread over the wing material back to the bend of the hook, then return-wind back to the starting point. This will give you an even base for the body. If the hair or feathers are not long enough to do this, tie in near the bend. If you are going to use tinsel for the body, it is best to build up any irregularities with tying thread so you have a smooth base for the tinsel. For tinsel bodies follow Diagram 47.

Diagrams 54, 55. Feather-wing streamers are tied three ways.

1. Select hackle (saddle or neck) of equal length and conformity. Strip off the stump end to the desired length. Place together so that the tip

ends are even. Grasp the stump ends between the thumb and index finger and spin so that the feathers flare. Tie in as previously described.

2. Select six to eight matching hackles (three or four for each side). Be sure to have their tips even. Place together so their concave sides face each other and tie on to the shank as described in Diagram 54.

3. Splay the wing. Select wings as described in the paragraph above. Place three or four together and bind their stump ends with tying thread as in Diagram 54. Take two wings and tie in so their convex sides are together (wings flare out). After bodies and wings are completed, the fly is finished by winding on hackle at the head of the fly as shown in Diagrams 54 and 55.

Mylar Tube Bodies

After the wings are tied in, pull the cords from the center of the mylar tubing. Your tying thread should be in back of the wing and at the bend of the hook. Push the mylar tubing over the eye of the hook, back to the bend, and secure with tying thread. Whip-finish and cut off the thread. Now cut off the tubing in back of the eye. Attach tying thread and tie in the front end of the tubing. Lacquer the exposed tying thread where the tubing has been secured. Finish the fly as illustrated in Diagram 54.

Diagram 56. Deer-hair wings may be tied in as shown. All other steps are carried out as previously described.

17
Harvey's Night Fly

~~~~~~~~~

THIS is the fly that has taken more large trout for me than all other flies combined. The method of fishing this fly is described in the chapter on techniques. I tie the fly on large hooks, sizes 4 to 2/0.

Diagram 57. Following Diagram 17, tie in the tail and hackle for ribbing. Dub heavily for the body. Wind the dubbing up close to the eye but end this body abruptly. This will give you a wedge to help flare out the wings as shown. After palmering is completed, tie in another hackle and wind on tight against the body. Now select two matching heavy-quilled breast feathers. I use goose or duck depending on the size of the hook. Wings should be long enough to reach back to the bend of the hook. I don't believe color makes much difference with the night flies; however, I am a little partial to the darker colors.

Tie the wings so they flare out at the sides as illustrated.

DIAGRAM 57

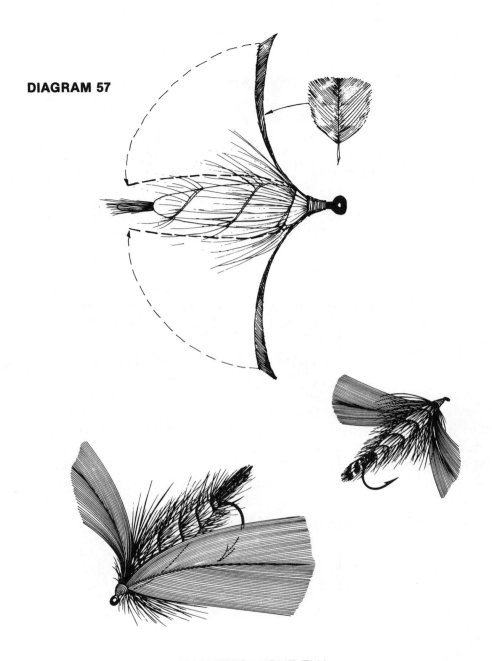

HARVEY'S NIGHT FLY

18

Bass Bugs

～～～～～～

THE name bass bug is quite misleading to the tyer. He usually associates these lures with the largemouth and smallmouth black bass. It is quite true these lures were first constructed to take bass but now are universally used for all species of fresh- or saltwater fish that will take a lure on the surface of the water. Considering the great number of fish that will strike these large fly-rod bugs, it is only natural there should be countless numbers on the market today.

There is one characteristic that distinguishes the bugs from fly-rod plugs. Hair or feathers used separately or together are part of the construction of the bugs, whereas fly-rod plugs are usually made conspicuous by their absence.

Any fly tyer who is able to tie trout flies will find the bass bugs quite simple to make. Even though there are different patterns, the techniques of constructing these various lures are quite similar. In this explanation I will cover only hair-bodied and cork-bodied lures. They are typical examples and the tyer who can tie or construct the ones illustrated should be able to imitate any of the others without too much difficulty.

There are a few important fundamentals that should be remembered when making bugs. First, be sure you have sufficient hooking space. By this I mean plenty of space between the body and the barb of the hook. If too little of the gap is exposed it is very difficult to hook the fish. In addition, the bug in most cases will not ride as it should, that is, with the hook in the water.

When tying bugs for your own use, construct them so they will work well with the rod, or rods, with which you intend to fish. There is nothing more annoying than to try to fish with bugs so large they cannot be manipulated or cast properly. Beginners commonly make this mistake.

DIAGRAM 58

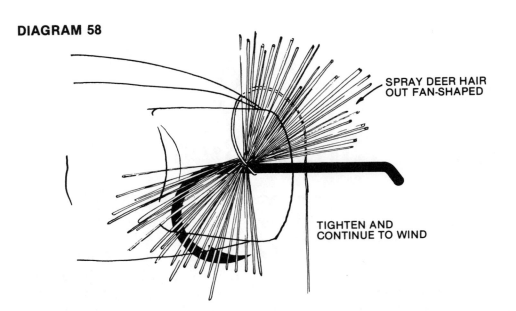

SPRAY DEER HAIR
OUT FAN-SHAPED

TIGHTEN AND
CONTINUE TO WIND

DIAGRAM 59

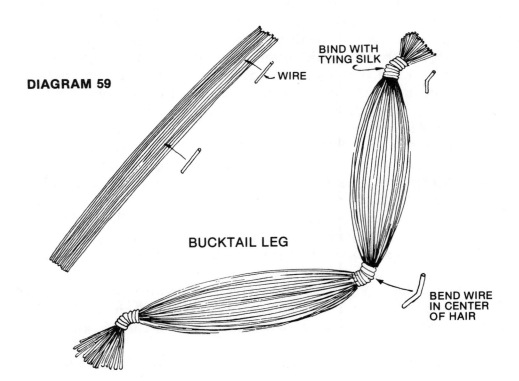

WIRE

BIND WITH
TYING SILK

BUCKTAIL LEG

BEND WIRE
IN CENTER
OF HAIR

Hollow-Hair Bugs

Antelope, caribou, deer, elk, moose, and reindeer all have hollow hair that can be used for hair bugs; however, one must remember that all hair from any one hide does not spin on equally well. This is especially true with whitetail-deer hair. Select only the coarsest hair. Hair from the neck and back is quite fine and for the beginner nearly impossible to spin, but is excellent for the wings. Beginners should remember that any hollow hair will spin easier on the bare shank of the hook than it will if the shank is covered with tying thread. The size of the tying thread used is usually determined by the size of the bunches of hair to be spun on the hook. The more hair one uses, the heavier the thread must be, and vice versa. Be sure the thread is heavy enough for the work you want it to do. It is well for the beginner to practice spinning on the hair before starting to tie hair bugs. Practice until the hair spins on smoothly and evenly around the shank of the hook.

Diagram 58 illustrates how this is done. First, secure the tying thread at the bend of the hook. Cut a small bunch of hair from the hide and hold it on the hook as illustrated. Spread the hair out into a fan shape by shifting thumb and index finger. Now take one or two (I prefer one) loose turns of tying thread around the hair where it is in contact with the hook. Draw up the tying thread until the hair starts to flare out, then let go of the hair and quickly make several more turns, passing the thread among the hairs. Now wind the tying thread to the front of the hair. Next, hold at the rear of the spun hair with the thumb and index finger of the left hand to keep the hair from moving on the shank. With the thumb and index finger of the right hand, push the hair together so that it will be as compact as possible. Repeat this process until the shank of the hook is covered or until you are satisfied you have mastered the technique.

Diagram 59. This diagram illustrates one method of making legs for a hair frog. Here deer tail hair is used. Select hair long enough for the legs, then pull out all the short hairs and even up the long ones. Take a piece of spring-steel wire and insert it in the center of the hair as illustrated. Wind over tightly as illustrated, lacquer, and bend as desired. Some tyers only insert wire in the knee joint, other tyers insert wire in all joints. The illustration shows my preference. This diagram shows only one leg; of course, two are needed.

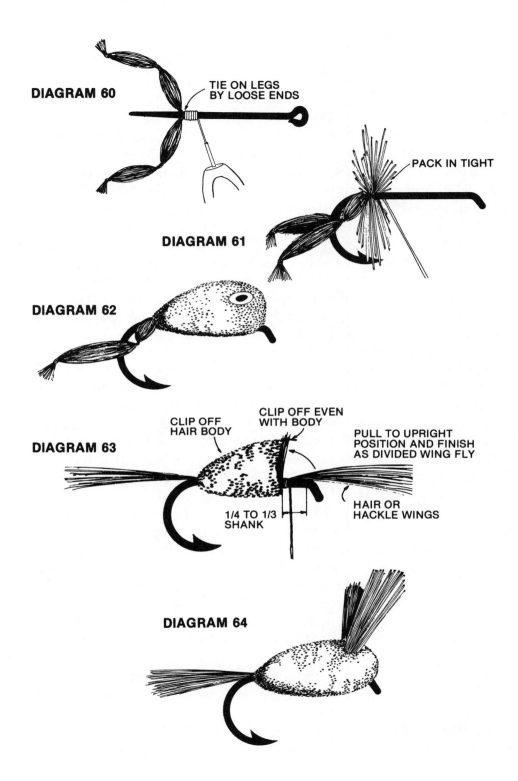

DIAGRAM 60

TIE ON LEGS BY LOOSE ENDS

DIAGRAM 61

PACK IN TIGHT

DIAGRAM 62

DIAGRAM 63

CLIP OFF HAIR BODY

CLIP OFF EVEN WITH BODY

PULL TO UPRIGHT POSITION AND FINISH AS DIVIDED WING FLY

1/4 TO 1/3 SHANK

HAIR OR HACKLE WINGS

DIAGRAM 64

Diagram 60. This diagram illustrates how and where the legs are tied on the hook. Secure the tying thread just in front of the bend, then lacquer. Now tie the top end of each leg to the hook. After the legs are secured, you may run the tying thread to the rear of the legs and wedge the thread tight against the legs to make them stand out at a wider angle. This spread is optional. Cover all windings with cement.

Diagram 61. This diagram shows the first bunch of hair spun on the hook after the legs have been tied on. I might add that the first bunch or two of hair is the most difficult to spin on smoothly because of the tying thread on the shank. Be sure the hair is packed tight up against the legs. Repeat this operation, spinning hair until the bare shank is covered with the desired amount. It is a good idea to apply a drop of lacquer or liquid cement to the shank where the hair makes contact after each bunch of hair is spun on. This will help keep it from twisting on the hook.

Diagram 62. One may go all out with his artistic sense when trimming hair frogs. I have never found that looks added very much to the fish-taking qualities of the frog. Diagram 62 just suggests one shape to trim the frog. Eyes may be added or built up with plastic and painted as desired.

Diagram 63. This diagram illustrates proportioning of hair bugs. A single tail is tied on, then hair is spun on up to one-fourth or one-third the distance from the eye. Trim to the desired shape. Tie in wings as illustrated. Wings are then divided as shown in Diagram 31. Spin additional hair up to the eye of the hook and trim.

Diagram 64. Some tyers spin on exceptionally long hair when they get to the point where they want the wings, then when trimming the body they just leave bunches of long hair for the wings. If the hair is uneven, it may be trimmed as illustrated. The wings may be tied or clipped at any angle on the body.

Cork-Bodied Bugs

Diagrams 65, 66. One may purchase cork cylinders in various shapes and sizes. Although bodies can be shaped by hand from cork cylinders, I prefer to buy the ones already shaped. You can still make changes on the face if you wish.

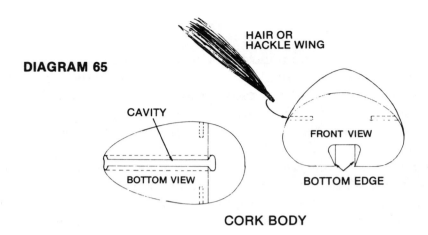

DIAGRAM 65

HAIR OR
HACKLE WING

CAVITY

FRONT VIEW

BOTTOM VIEW

BOTTOM EDGE

CORK BODY

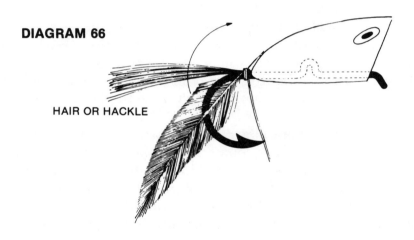

DIAGRAM 66

HAIR OR HACKLE

DIAGRAM 67

BEND HAIRWING
BACK AND TIE OVER
TOP TO HOLD DOWN

TAIL TIED
ON FIRST

If you are going to make a number of bugs it is best to prepare all the cork bodies in advance. Diagram 65 illustrates the method I use. I cut the slots with a sharp razor blade or scalpel. Make the entrance to the slot just big enough to slip in the hump-shanked hook; if you don't, the body will turn on the hook. If the bug is to have a tail, cover the shank of the hook with Shoe Goo solution or any other cement, then wind the tying thread from the eye to the bend to give a base that is better than just a bare hook. Tie in a tail about as long as in Diagram 66. Cement on the body.

Many different cements are available but be sure to use one of good quality. I mix plastic wood and cement together. Fill the cavity, then insert the hook. Next, I pack and smooth off the surface and ends of the cavity. Allow it to set for at least twenty-four hours, then smooth off the surface with fine sandpaper or an emery board. If the cork is pitted it should be given a coat or two of filler. Now you can spray or paint with lacquer any desired color or combination of colors.

Diagram 67. Some bugs have wings on top. Diagram 67 shows how they are attached. If the wings are on the side of the bug, small holes may be drilled in the side and ends of wings wrapped with the tying thread. Fill the cavities with cement and insert wings as in Diagram 65.

Spent wings that are too long and heavy will be difficult to cast and in addition the bug may not ride the water as it should. It is always best to experiment before making a great number.

In conclusion, let me suggest the beginner keep his bugs on the small size. They will be simpler to construct and easier to cast as well as more enjoyable to fish.

19
Deer-Hair Terrestrials

~~~~~~~~

Diagrams 68, 69, 70. Clipped deer-hair terrestrials are tied the same as the deer-hair bass bugs. Diagrams 68, 69, and 70 show the green inchworm, Japanese beetle, and cricket. Use 2X long and regular-shank hooks in size #10 and #12 for the inchworm. Use #10 short-shank for the Japanese beetle, and regular-length shank sizes #8, #10, and #12 for the cricket.

Green Inchworm

Spin on dyed medium-light-green deer hair. Clip to approximately the proportion shown in Diagram 68. To accentuate the segmentation you make take a few turns around each indentation with green tying silk. Although it is not necessary, you may finish each one with a whip-finish.

Japanese Beetle

Spin black deer hair on a short-shank hook, pack firmly. Clip as illustrated in Diagram 69. You may tie on, or cement, a jungle-cock eye on the top, or tie on the top a burnt fluorescent wing (I use hot pink). I use this wing on the cricket, deer-hair ant, and caddis. After tying on the wing, tie on each side three thick deer hairs for legs. Cut off at the appropriate length. This will enable you to follow the bug, even in heavy, riffly water.

DIAGRAM 68

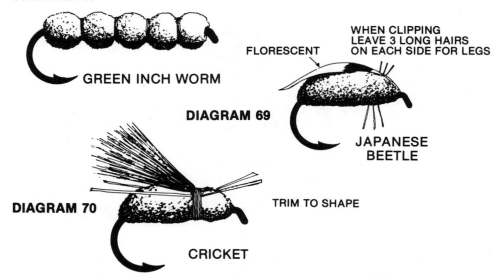

GREEN INCH WORM

FLORESCENT

WHEN CLIPPING
LEAVE 3 LONG HAIRS
ON EACH SIDE FOR LEGS

DIAGRAM 69

JAPANESE
BEETLE

DIAGRAM 70

TRIM TO SHAPE

CRICKET

DEER HAIR ANT

DIAGRAM 71

TIE HAIR ON
HOOK SHANK AND
SPIRAL BELOW BEND

DIAGRAM 72

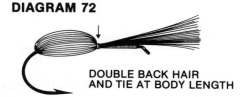

DOUBLE BACK HAIR
AND TIE AT BODY LENGTH

DIAGRAM 73

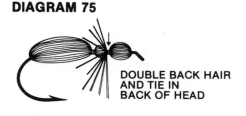

TIE IN SMALL SEGMENT
BEHIND HEAD, TIE IN
AGAIN BEHIND EYE

DIAGRAM 74

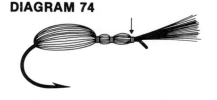

DOUBLE BACK HAIR
AND TIE IN
BACK OF HEAD

DIAGRAM 75

DIAGRAM 76

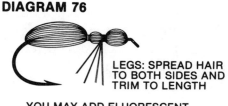

LEGS: SPREAD HAIR
TO BOTH SIDES AND
TRIM TO LENGTH

YOU MAY ADD FLUORESCENT
YARN TO TOP FOR
VISABILITY ON WATER

Cricket

Spin black deer hair and clip as in Diagram 70. Take a bunch of black deer hair and tie on top, about one-third the distance back from the eye. After tying on the wing, take black goose-quill fibers and tie one on each side for the legs, as shown in the illustration.

Deerhair Ant

Many variations may be used when tying floating deer-hair ants and beetles. The one illustrated and described is the simplest to tie. Use hook sizes #10 and #20. Coat the shank of the hook with Shoe Goo. This will help keep the hair from twisting on the hook. Wind on your tying thread from the eye back to the bend of the hook, then reverse and wind back to the middle of the shank. Cut a bunch of black or brown deer hair and pull out all the short hairs. Even up the long hairs. The hair should be at least two and one-half times as long as the hook. Tie in the stump end of the hair at about the center of the shank. Spiral the tying thread back over the hair to the bend of the hook, pull the hair back, and secure with four or five turns of the thread as shown in **Diagram 71.** Spiral the tying thread up to the center of the shank, pull the deer hair forward and secure as in **Diagram 72.** Be sure to keep the hair evenly distributed. Now wind the thread up a few turns, pull hair forward, and bind again (**Diagram 73**). Wind the tying thread to a point behind the eye and secure as in **Diagram 74.** Bring the thread back in front of the thorax and pull hair back and tie down as in **Diagram 75.** Bring the thread immediately to the eye and tie off. Pull three or four hairs out on each side for legs then cut off the rest of the hair (**Diagram 76**). Cut off the legs to the desired length, then coat all exposed thread with cement.

You have now covered all the necessary steps to tie any fly you wish. Any new pattern, with a few changes, will be simple to tie if you have a model. You no doubt will come up with some techniques that will be best for you. I sincerely hope you will enjoy this hobby and will teach others to tie their own flies. This is the best way I know to promote fly fishing. Good luck!

Three

Appendices

ANGLER'S KNOTS

BLOOD KNOT — To tie strands of equal diameter

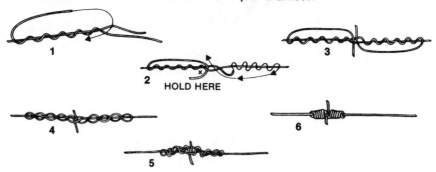

IMPROVED BLOOD KNOT — To tie strands of unequal diameter

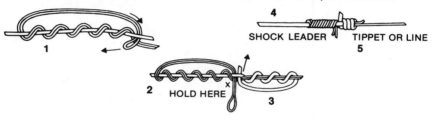

SURGEON'S KNOT — To tie strands of unequal diameter

HARVEY'S DOUBLE SLIP KNOT — To tie leader to hook

IMPROVED CLINCH KNOT — To tie lure or hook to leader

PERFECTION LOOP KNOT — To tie loop in end of leader

 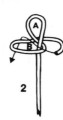 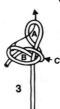 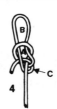 

1   2   3   4   5

DOUBLE TURLE KNOT — To tie your fly to tippet

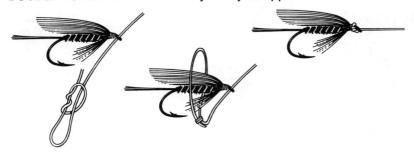

NAIL KNOT — To tie leader to line

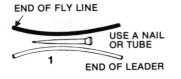

END OF FLY LINE

USE A NAIL OR TUBE

1

END OF LEADER

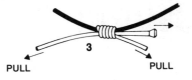

3

PULL   PULL

END OF FLY LINE

2

LEADER END

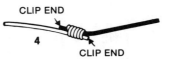

CLIP END

4

CLIP END

DRY AND WET FLY PATTERNS

PATTERN	WINGS	HACKLE	BODY	TAIL
ADAMS (male) D	Grizzly tips, tied spent wings	Brown and grizzly	Gray dubbing or muskrat fur	Brown and grizzly
ADAMS (yellow) D	Grizzly tips, tied spent wings	Brown and grizzly	Yellow dubbing	Brown and grizzly
ALDER Flat Wing DW	Brown turkey tied flat over back	Black	Peacock herl, gold tip	
ALDER Ronalds W	Speckled hen tied close to shank	Brown	Bronze peacock herl	
ALEXANDRIA #1 W	Peacock sword	Black	Embossed silver, red floss tip	Peacock herl or sword
BADGER BIVISIBLE D		Light badger, Palmer		Light badger hackle tip
BADGER QUILL D	Slate	Badger	Peacock quill	Badger hackle
BADGER SPIDER D		Badger	Black chenille	Badger
BEAVERKILL (female) D	Slate (light)	Brown	Gray dubbing, yellow chenille	Badger
BLACK ANGEL D	Black hackle tips	Black	Black, smooth floss	Black hackles
BLACK ANT W		Black	Black floss lacquered (or plastic) tied on inhump hook (knobbed at rear)	No tail
BLACK GNAT DW	Dark gray	Black	Black chenille, silver tip	With or without red fibers
BLACK MIDGE D		Black	Black floss, silver rib	
BLACK NYMPH W		Partridge	Black herl, gold rib	Wood duck
BLACK QUILL DW	Dark gray	Black	Peacock eye quill	Black
BLACK QUILL DUN D	Black	Black	Peacock herl quill	Coch-y-bondhu
BLUE DUN D	Pale gray	Pale blue dun	Pale blue fur	Pale blue dun
BLUE FOX D	Grizzly hackle tips	Grizzly	Blue dun fox dubbing	Grizzly hackle
BLUE HONEY DUN D	Wood duck	Blue honey dun	Buff fox fur dubbing	Blue honey dun hackle
BLUE QUILL DW	Medium gray	Blue dun	Peacock quill	Blue dun hackle
BLUE QUILL VARIANT D	Blue dun hackle tips	Blue dun, long spider	Peacock quill	Blue dun hackle fibers
BLUE WING OLIVE D	Blue dun hackle tips	Golden brown	Olive green dubbing	Brown hackle
BLUE WING OLIVE D (female)	Bluish gray	Olive	Brown floss, olive thread rib	Dark-olive-brown hackle
BREADCRUST D		Grizzly	Rhode Island Red quill hackle	
BROWN HACKLE DW		Brown	Peacock herl gold tip	Gold pheasant tippet

BROWN MALLARD DW	Brown mallard	Brown	Brown dubbing picked out, gold rib	Brown mallard
BROWN NYMPH W		Chestnut partridge	Brown herl	Wood duck
CAHILL-Dark DW	Wood duck	Brown	Muskrat or hare's fur dubbing, gold tip	Wood duck
CAHILL-Light DW	Wood duck	Light ginger	Red fox belly fur (cream)	Wood duck
CARMICHAEL D	Grizzly hackle tips spent	Brown/grizzly mixed	Pink fur	Brown neck guard hackle
COACHMAN DW	White	Brown	Peacock herl gold tip	
COACHMAN-CABIN DW	Andalusian hackle tips	Grizzly and brown	Peacock herl	Red hackle fibers
COACHMAN LEADWING DW (or dark)	Gray duck, dark	Brown	Peacock herl, gold tip	Gold pheasant tippet
COACHMAN ROYAL DW	White	Brown	Peacock herl, red floss	Gold pheasant
COWDUNG DW	White dyed light brown	Brown	Olive floss, gold tip	
DARK OLIVE DUN D (female)	Blue dun	Dark blue dun	Blue quill, gold rib and tip	Olive green hackle
DARK OLIVE DUN D (male)	Blue dun	Dark blue dun	Blue floss, brown thread rib	Dark olive hackle
DARK SEDGE D		Blood red	Dark green dubbing, gold wire rib	
DONELLY VARIANT D	Badger hackle tips	Brown/grizzly mixed	Muskrat fur	Brown throat guard hackle fiber
DUSTY MILLER D	Gray turkey	Grizzly	Gray dubbing, gold tip	Brown hackle
FISH HAWK D	Brown turkey, jungle cock eye	Brown	Gold, brown thread rib	Brown turkey
GINGER QUILL Light DW	Light gray	Ginger	Peacock quill (light)	Ginger
GORDON QUILL DW	Wood duck	Blue dun	Peacock quill, gold wire rib	Blue dun
GRANNOM D	Dark brown turkey	Brown	Brown dubbing, bright green butt	Blunt green tail
GRAY HACKLE - Peacock DW		Grizzly	Peacock herl, gold tip	Gold pheasant
GREEN DRAKE-Harvey D	Dyed yellow calf tail	Golden badger	Pale yellow spun fur	Black skunk tail
GRIZZLY KING D	Gray mallard, red strips	Grizzly	Green floss, gold rib and tip	Scarlet hackle
HARE'S EAR - Gold Rib DW	Gray		Hare's ear dubbing picked out, gold rib and tip	Rabbit hair
HARVEY'S SPECIAL W	Mottled brown turkey	Black	Muskrat dyed black	Black
HENDRICKSON-Dark DW	Dark wood duck	Dark blue dun	Dark fox belly fur	Wood duck
HENDRICKSON-Light DW (original)	Wood duck	Blue dun, pale	Light fox belly fur (cream)	Wood duck
IRON BLUE DUN D	COOT	Iron blue dun	Brown and deep red dubbing mixed	Iron blue dun
JASID D	Jungle cock eye	Any color	Any color floss body ribbed with same hackle used on front	

PATTERN	WINGS	HACKLE	BODY	TAIL
LIGHT FOX D	Dark gray	Yellow	White dubbing picked out, yellow tag, gold tip	
MARCH BROWN DW	Dark brown turkey	Brown	Gray-brown dubbing, yellow floss rib, gold tip	Brown hackle
OLIVE DUN D	Light blue gray	Olive dun	Olive dubbing, gold rib	Olive dun hackle
PALE EVENING DUN D	Light gray	White	Cream-yellow dubbing, gold tip	White hackle
PALE SULPHUR D	Palest cream	Palest yellow	Palest yellow dubbing	Palest yellow hackle
PINK LANDY Winged D	Gray	Ginger	Pink floss, gold rib and tip	
RED QUILL DW	Gray	Natural dark red	Red peacock quill (dyed)	Natural dark red
ROYAL COACHMAN DW	White	Brown	Peacock herl, red floss center joint	Golden pheasant tippet
SPRUCE CREEK D	Wood duck	Black or dark blue dun	Dark peacock sword quill	Black
SULPHUR - Harvey	White hackle tips	Light ginger and light orange mixed	Rabbit fur yellow, orange pink and white mixed	
TRICO DUN D	White	Light blue dun	Green-olive dubbing	Light blue dun
TRICO SPINNER D	Polypropylene		Black dyed muskrat	Black
TUP'S INDISPENSABLE D		Honey dun	Yellow	Honey Dun
WHIRLING BLUE DUN D	Dark gray	Ginger-brown	Blue-gray dubbing, gold tip	Brown hackle
WICKHAM'S FANCY D	Slate gray quill	Brown, brown Palmer	Gold tinsel	Brown Hackle

BUCKTAIL AND STREAMER PATTERNS

TOPPING — CHEEK — EYE — HACKLE — WING — TAIL — BODY

PATTERN	WINGS	HACKLE	BODY	TAIL
BLACK DOSE	2 black saddles in center, 2 red grizzly saddles outside	Red grizzly	Black wool, silver rib	Gold pheasant crest
BLACK GHOST	4 white saddles	Yellow feathers at throat	Black floss, silver rib	Yellow feather
BLACK MARABOU	Black marabou, red feather, cheek, peacock herl topping		Gold	
BLACK AND YELLOW	Black bucktail over yellow		Silver	Gold pheasant crest
BROWN GHOST	Brown neck hackles, gold pheasant crest topping	Yellow	Brown floss, gold rib	Gold pheasant crest

COSSEBOOM	Gray squirrel	Yellow		Light green wool, silver rib	Light green wool
GRAY GHOST	Blue dun neck hackle, silver pheasant breat shoulder, jungle cock eye cheek	Sparse white bucktail under hook, 5 or 6 strands of peacock herl, last, sparse yellow	Orange floss, silver rib		
GREEN GHOST	Green saddles or neck hackles, silver pheasant breat feather shoulder, jungle cock eye cheek	Sparse white bucktail under hook, 5 or 6 strands of peacock herl first, gold pheasant crest fastened at throat	Orange floss, silver rib		
JUNGLE SUPERVISOR	White hair, 2 blue saddles on top, jungle cock eye shoulder		Silver, silver wire rib		Red feather
LADY GHOST	Badger, copper pheasant shoulder, gold pheasant crest topping	Peacock herl and white hair long, gold pheasant crest fastened at throat	Silver, oval silver rib		Gold pheasant tippet
MATUKA	2 hen saddles	Same as wing, rib over wing with gold wire or tinsel	Any selected color		
MICKEY FINN	Yellow over red over yellow hair		Silver, silver twist rib		
TIGER-Dark	Brown bucktail, peacock herl topping, jungle cock eye shoulder	Red feather (short) at throat	Yellow chenille, silver tip		Barred wood duck
TIGER-Light	Pale yellow hair, short red feater on top, jungle cock eye shoulder		Peacock herl, silver tip		Barred wood duck
WARDEN'S WONDER	Red grizzly	Yellow (full)	Silver		Red wood tail tag
WHITE MARABOU	White marabou, red feather cheek, peacock herl topping		Gold		
WOOLLY BUGGER		Black	Black, olive or brown palmered with black hackle		Black marabou
YELLOW MARABOU	Yellow marabou, red feather cheek, peacock herl topping		Gold		

Bleaching Instructions

~~~~~~~~

ANY material used in fly tying can be bleached to a lighter shade by using the following solution.

Ingredients: CLAIROXIDE (20 volume solution of hydrogen peroxide with ammonia), available at most drug stores.

CLAIROL, Extra-strength basic white powder lightener, available through a beautician's supply house.

Directions:
1. Mix one tablespoon of Clairol to each ounce of Clairoxide.
2. Submerge materials until desired shade is reached and immediately rinse in cold water.
3. Do not keep materials in solution for more than one hour.